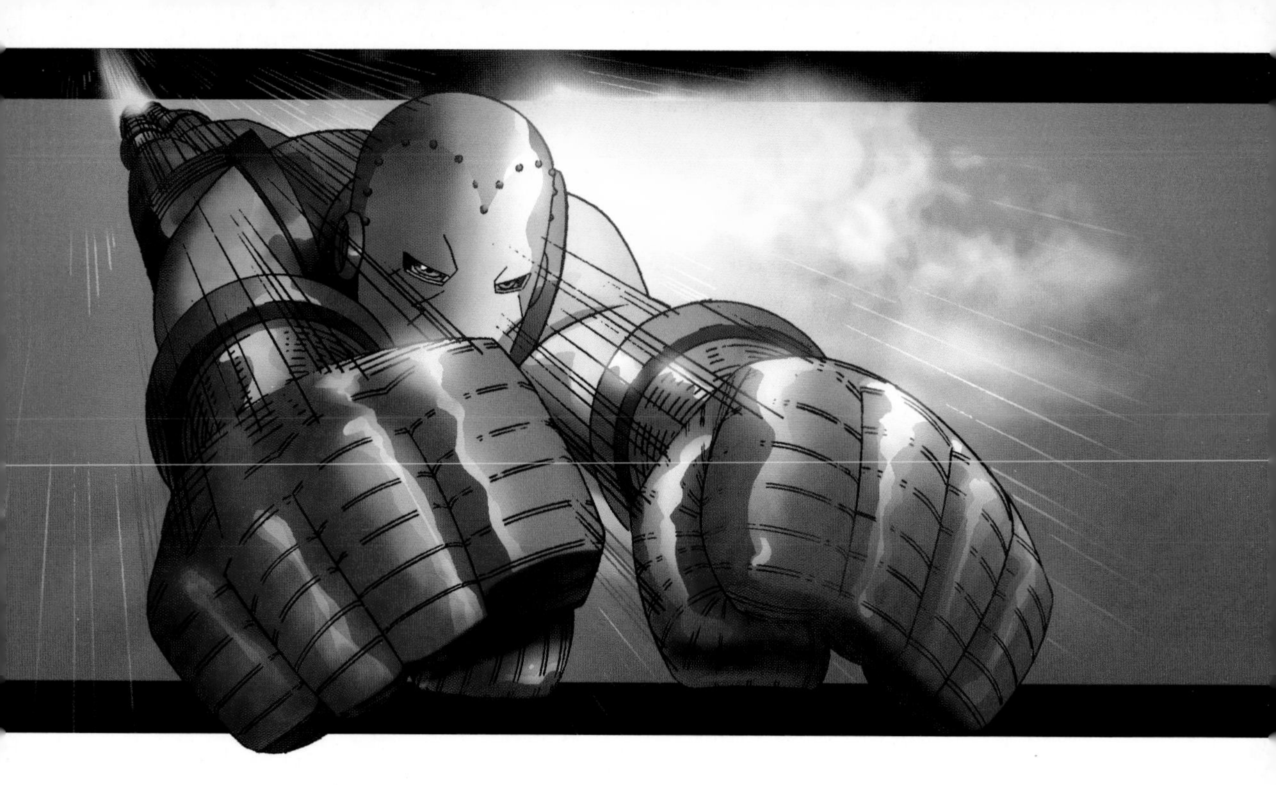

EARTH'S MIGHTIEST HEROES

WRITER:
JOE CASEY

ART:
SCOTT KOLINS

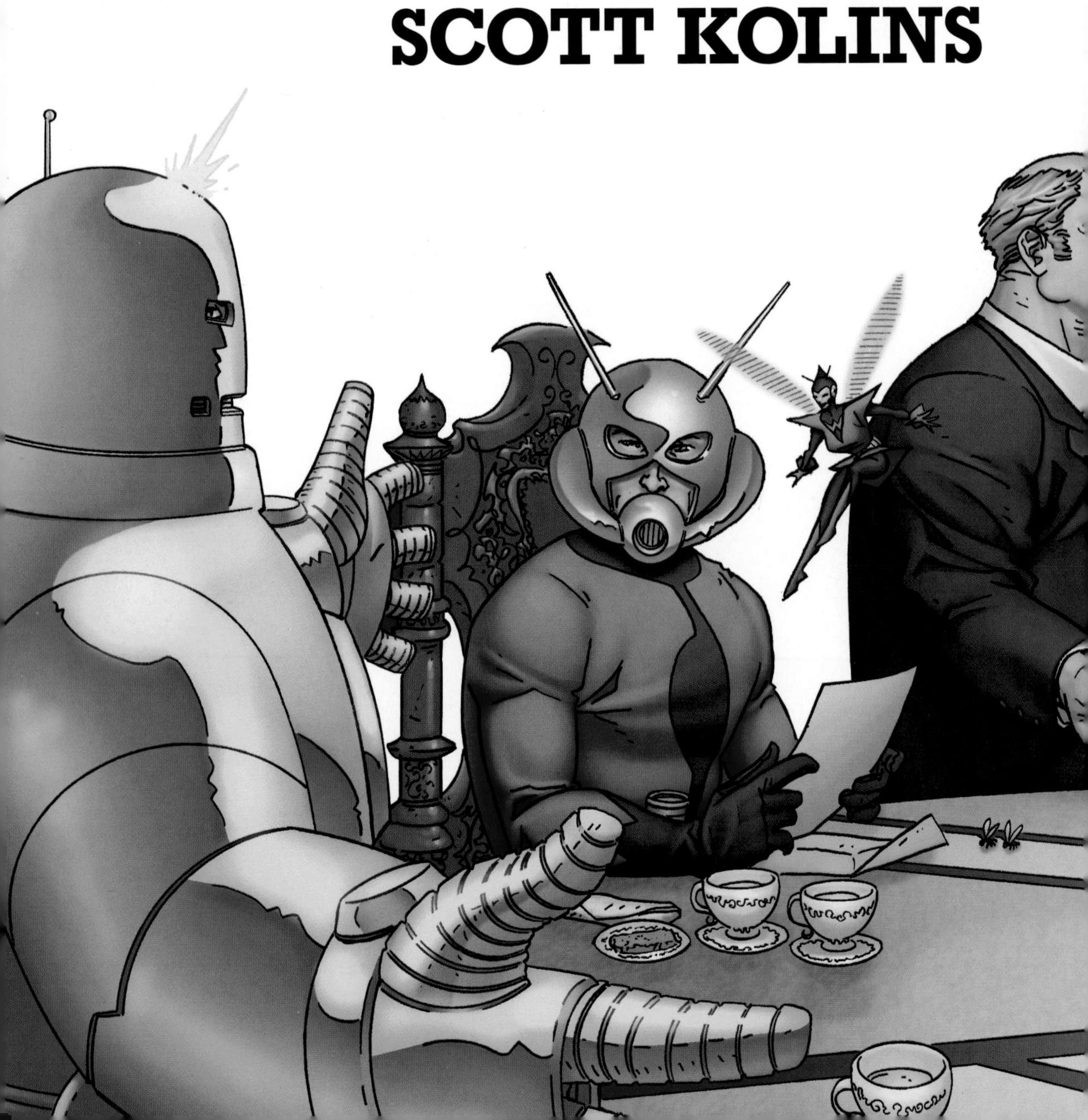

COLOR ART: Morry Hollowell & Wil Quintana
LETTERS: Richard Starkings & Comicraft
ASSISTANT EDITORS: Andy Schmidt, Nicole Wiley & Molly Lazer
EDITOR: Tom Brevoort

COLLECTION EDITOR: Mark D. Beazley
ASSISTANT EDITOR: Jennifer Grünwald
SENIOR EDITOR, SPECIAL PROJECTS: Jeff Youngquist
PRODUCTION: Ternard Solomon
BOOK DESIGNER: Patrick McGrath
CREATIVE DIRECTOR: Tom Marvelli

EDITOR IN CHIEF: Joe Quesada
PUBLISHER: Dan Buckley

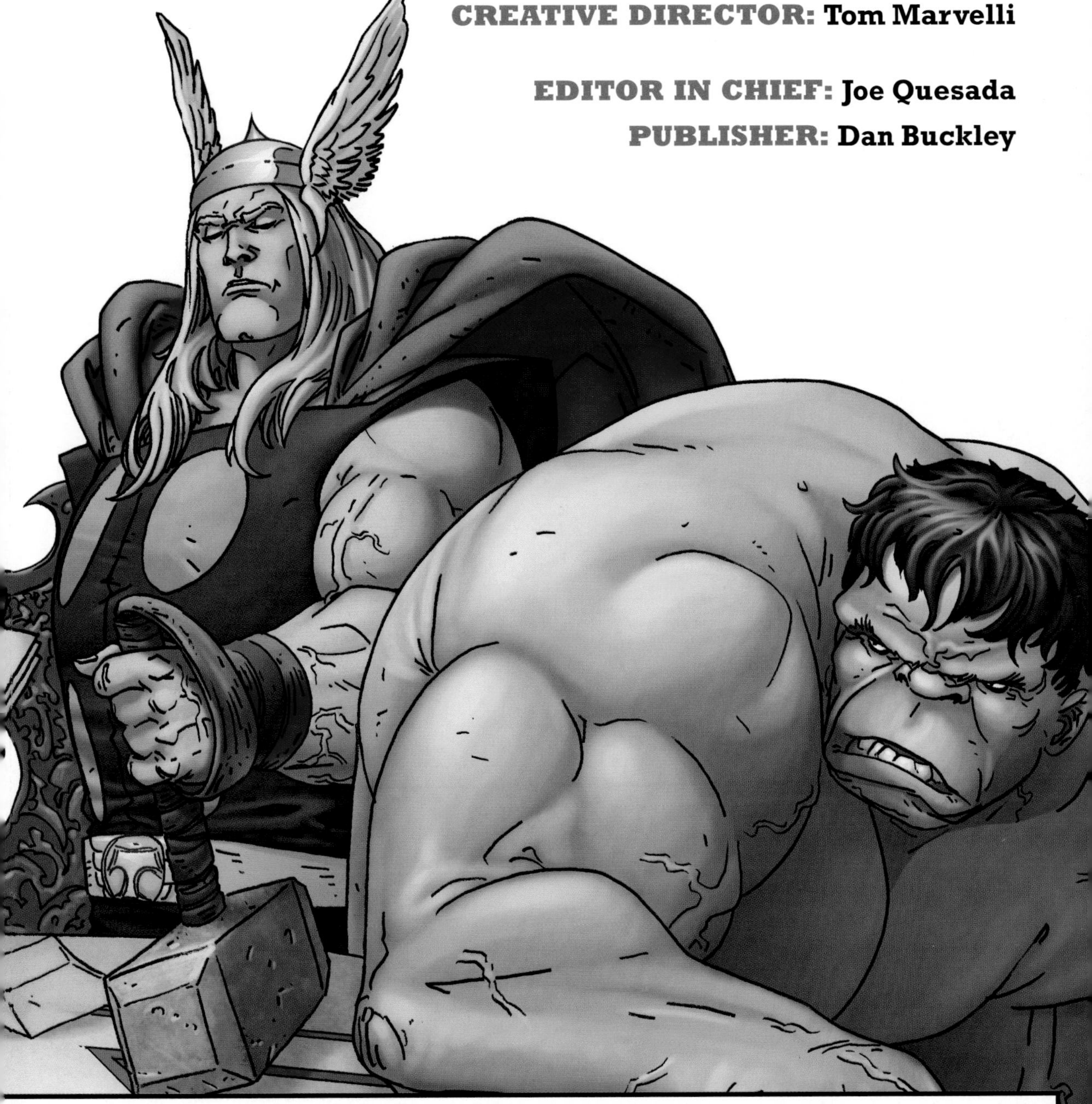

AVENGERS: EARTH'S MIGHTIEST HEROES. Contains material originally published in magazine form as AVENGERS: EARTH'S MIGHTIEST HEROES #1-8. First printing 2005. ISBN# 0-7851-1438-6. Published by MARVEL COMICS, a division of MARVEL ENTERTAINMENT GROUP, INC. OFFICE OF PUBLICATION: 10 East 40th Street, New York, NY 10016. $24.99 per copy in the U.S. and $40.00 in Canada (GST #R127032852); Canadian Agreement #40668537. **Printed in the U.S.A.** AVI ARAD, Chief Creative Officer; ALAN FINE, President & CEO of Toy Biz and Marvel Publishing; DAN CARR, Director of Production; ELAINE CALLENDER, Director of Manufacturing; DAVID BOGART, Managing Editor; STAN LEE, Chairman Emeritus. For information regarding advertising in Marvel Comics or on Marvel.com, please contact Joe Maimone, Advertising Director, at jmaimone@marvel.com or 212-576-8534.

10 9 8 7 6 5 4 3 2 1

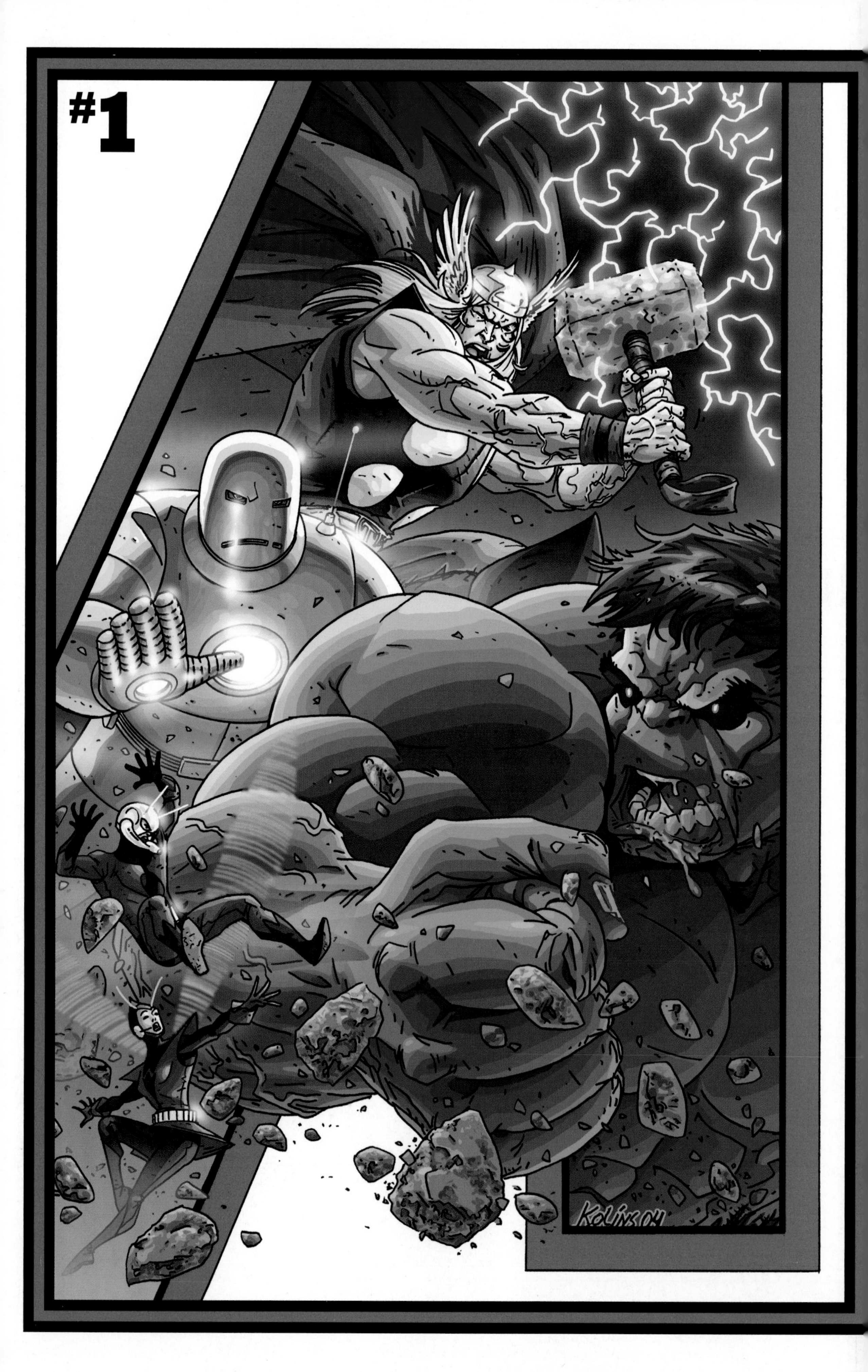
#1
KOLINS 04

STARK INDUSTRIES FLUSHING, N.Y.
...PER YOUR INSTRUCTIONS, I'VE SENT A COPY OF THE BY-LAWS TO AGENT MURCH.
THE ORIGINAL WAS SENT BY ARMED COURIER TO THE MANSION...
FANTASTIC. THANK YOU, PEPPER.
REMEMBER, YOU STILL NEED TO MEET WITH MISTER CATON IN ACCOUNTING ON THE FUNDING ISSUE.
OFFICIAL CHARTER
GOOD NIGHT, MISTER STARK.

... EVEN MORE QUESTIONS ABOUT THE NATURE OF THIS NEW ENDEAVOR, IN WHICH FIVE SUPER-POWERED BEINGS HAVE ANNOUNCED THEIR INTENTION TO BAND TOGETHER IN AN OFFICIAL CAPACITY.
THE PRESIDENT IS EXPECTED TO COMMENT LATER TONIGHT...
C'MON, VINNIE... TIME FOR A GUT CHECK.
ONE SHOT? ALL YOUR BALLS... IN ONE SHOT?!
YOU GOT A BET, BARTON.
TED BAILS IS LIVE ON FIFTH AVENUE. TED...?
MIA, BEHIND ME SITS THE MANSION BUILT IN 1932 BY HOWARD STARK... NOW OWNED BY HIS GRANDSON, ANTHONY, CEO OF STARK INDUSTRIES.
STARK'S BODYGUARD HAS, SO FAR, BEEN THE PUBLIC FACE OF THIS NEWLY ANNOUNCED ORGANIZATION, AS WELL AS BEING A FOUNDING MEMBER. OTHER MEMBERS HAVE BEEN ARRIVING THROUGHOUT THE DAY...
THE MYSTERIOUS INDIVIDUAL KNOWN ONLY AS THOR ARRIVED AT THE MANSION THIS AFTERNOON, BUT HIS APPEARANCE PALED IN COMPARISON TO WHO SOON FOLLOWED...
EARLIER TODAY
TOO EASY...

GUH...
YOU TRYIN' TO CATCH FLIES THERE...?
GUESS I'LL HAVE A BEER ON YOU, STINKY.
PERHAPS THE MOST CONTROVERSIAL MEMBER WAS CAPTURED IN THIS AMATEUR VIDEO FOOTAGE AS HE LITERALLY LANDED ON 71ST STREET...
EARLIER TODAY
THE HULK HAS HAD SEVERAL RUN-INS WITH THE U.S. MILITARY IN THE PAST FEW MONTHS, AND A RECENT RAMPAGE IN A DETROIT AUTO PLANT SEEMED TO SERVE AS THE CATALYST FOR THIS GATHERING. STILL, HIS APPEARANCE AT THIS MEETING IS SURE TO RAISE EYEBROWS...
...THIS, DESPITE IRON MAN'S ASSURANCES DURING A PRESS CONFERENCE AT STARK INDUSTRIES YESTERDAY...
WHATEVER'S ON TAP, SID...
THE HULK IS NOT A MENACE. HIS RECENT PRESIDENTIAL PARDON MERELY REINFORCES OUR POSITION.
HE IS ONE OF US.
YESTERDAY

WE'RE WILLING TO STAKE OUR BURGEONING REPUTATIONS ON HIS VIRTUES AS A HERO...
BAD MOVE, TINHORN.
HERE YA GO, CLINT.
SO, HOW 'BOUT IT, SID? THINK THESE GUYS ARE ON THE LEVEL...?
YOU FIRST.
WELL, I'M NOT SURE I'M INTO THE WHOLE ELITIST VIBE THEY'VE GOT GOING ON. THE MANSION... STARK'S BODYGUARD SPEARHEADING THE THING...
POLITICAL PUNDITS ARE OFFERING THEIR ANALYSIS...
IT'S WORSE THAN THAT, KID. THAT IS SERIOUS POWER HOLING UP IN THAT HOUSE. WHO'S TO STOP 'EM FROM, I DUNNO... TAKIN' OVER COMPLETELY?!
YOU GONNA TAKE 'EM ON...?!
NOW THAT'S PESSIMISTIC.
Y'KNOW, THEY MIGHT JUST BE AS ALTRUISTIC AS THEY SAY THEY ARE.
THAT'D BE SOMETHING...
...AND THEIR HOPE IS THAT, IN THE COMING WEEKS, WE'LL ALL LEARN MORE ABOUT EXACTLY WHO THESE "AVENGERS" ARE.
RIGHT NOW, WE SIMPLY DON'T KNOW MUCH...

INTERESTING READING, JARVIS...?
VERY INTERESTING, SIR.
I CAN'T TELL IF THAT'S SARCASM OR NOT.
JUDGING BY THAT MEETING, I WOULDN'T BLAME YOU IF IT WAS...
CERTAINLY NOT.
IF I MAY, SIR... FOR FIVE HEADSTRONG PERSONALITIES TO FIND COMMON GROUND IS A FEAT IN ITSELF. AND NOT AN EASY ONE...
THAT'S FOR SURE...
TWO INSECT HEROES... ONE WHO CLAIMS GODHOOD... A LOUD-MOUTHED, UNCONTROLLABLE THUG...
... AND A RICH INDUSTRIALIST'S BODYGUARD.
QUITE THE MIX, EH?
I'LL PLACE THIS IN THE MAIN STUDY.
IT'S...A NOBLE DOCUMENT, SIR. IT WILL SURELY SERVE TO INSPIRE OTHERS.
I HOPE YOU'RE RIGHT.

-KOFF!-
-KAFF!-
SORRY ABOUT THAT, FOLKS. HE GETS... EMOTIONAL SOMETIMES. IF HE DIDN'T, HE WOULDN'T NEED ME HANGING AROUND, MAKING SURE HE DOESN'T SCREW UP AGAIN...
HE'LL COME AROUND, THOUGH. I'LL MAKE SURE OF IT. THIS IS TOO IMPORTANT...
LET'S HOPE SO, RICK...
I THINK THAT'S OUR CUE, IRON MAN.
I WOULDN'T CALL THIS MEETING A TOTAL DISASTER. THERE'S ALWAYS A LEARNING CURVE TO THESE THINGS. LET US KNOW WHEN THE COMPUTER SYSTEMS ARE UP AND RUNNING... I WANT TO NETWORK WITH MY LAB...
UNTIL NEXT TIME...!
"NOT A TOTAL DISASTER."
DON'T SWEAT IT. THIS IS LEGENDARY, MAN.
HEY...
...WHERE'D THOR GO?
-SIGH-
MEETING ADJOURNED.

DON'T PAY ANY ATTENTION TO HIM.
I'LL SIGN HIS NAME...
HEY!
YOU AIN'T MY AGENT, JONES!
DON'T BE STUPID, HULK.
THIS IS THE OPPORTUNITY OF A LIFETIME FOR YOU. UNLESS YOU WANT TO SPEND THE MAJORITY OF YOUR TIME SPARRING WITH THE MILITARY...!
WHO YOU CALLIN' "STUPID"?
HEY... C'MON, MAN--
YOU WANNA LOSE THOSE HANDS, KID?
DON'T YOU GET IT?! WE'RE GOING TO BAT FOR YOU! STAKING OUR REPUTATION ON --
WHO ASKED YA TO?
THIS BEHAVIOR...
...'TIS EGREGIOUS.
THOU SHALT BOTH STAND DOWN.
THOR...
STAY OUTTA THIS, CURLY. THIS IS BETWEEN ME AN' --
I DO NOT VOICE MY OPINION TWICE, BRUTE.
HUH.
SO THAT'S HOW IT IS.
I DON'T NEED THIS... FROM ANY OF YOU.

WELL, I'M CONVINCED.
THE SOONER WE CAN GET PAST THESE ADMINISTRATIVE HASSLES, THE SOONER WE CAN GET TO WORK FOR REAL.
HAND OVER THAT PEN WHEN YOU'RE DONE, HANDSOME.

THANK YOU BOTH.
I'M ANXIOUS TO GET STARTED, TOO.
ONCE I GET BACK TO THE NSC, OUR COMPUTER SYSTEMS WILL GO ONLINE, ALLOWING US TO CONSTANTLY MONITOR ACTIVITY WORLDWIDE...

I CAN'T BELIEVE YOU GUYS ARE REALLY DOING IT. AFTER DETROIT, I SURE WOULDN'T HAVE FIGURED ON ALL THIS...!
BUT IT'S GONNA BE AMAZING... AND TO THINK IT ALL STARTED WITH MY DISTRESS CALL...!
SO... I GOTTA WRITE... MY NAME...?

AND LET'S NOT FORGET THE ATTENDANT CELEBRITY THAT'LL COME WITH THIS JOB.
I MEAN, BETWEEN TONY STARK ON THE BUSINESS SIDE AND OUR VERY OWN NORSE GOD, WE'VE GOT A PRETTY PHOTOGENIC CREW HERE...

WASP, I CAN UNDERSTAND THE LURE OF FAME, BUT WE NEED TO KEEP THINGS IN PERSPECTIVE.
AND I DON'T WANT TO SEE ANYONE SIGNING ANY ENDORSEMENT DEALS. THAT'S NO WAY TO EARN THE PUBLIC'S TRUST.

YOU MEAN, LIKE WORKING FOR STARK INDUSTRIES, MAYBE...?
YOUR CONVICTION DOTH INSPIRE ME, IRON MAN.
LET THIS DAY COMMEMORATE A GREAT UNDERTAKING, AS WE EACH EARN OUR PLACE IN VALHALLA.
BIG TALK, FANCY PANTS.
FACT IS, WE AIN'T EVER GONNA GET THAT TRUST... FROM ANYONE.
AND I AIN'T SIGNIN' SQUAT.

WASP...?
THERE. MUCH BETTER.
I WAS JUST WONDERING...IS THIS LEGAL? I MEAN, BY SIGNING A BINDING CONTRACT --
IT'S NOT QUITE A CONTRACT, PER SE. THINK OF IT AS... A DECLARATION. A STATEMENT OF INTENT.
OUR INTENT.
ANT-MAN? WHAT DO YOU SAY?
YOU SURE YOU DON'T WANT ME TO READ THAT FOR YOU, BIG GUY...?
SHUDDUP.
SO, WHAT IS OUR INTENT, RUST-POT?
'TIS OBVIOUS.
WE SHALL COMBAT THE FOES NO SINGLE WARRIOR COULD EVER WITHSTAND. NO MATTER THE PERSONAL COST, 'TIS OUR DESTINY TO PROTECT THOSE IN NEED... THE INNOCENT, THE MEEK... ON THIS WORLD...
...AND WORLDS BEYOND.
UHHH...
RIGHT.
THAT'S... CERTAINLY ONE WAY TO PUT IT.

WHATEVER.
...AND I'M NOT THRILLED ABOUT GETTING INTO BED WITH THE NSC EITHER. BUT IT'S A NECESSARY EVIL IF WE'RE TO BE GRANTED A-1 SECURITY CLEARANCE...
...OTHERWISE KNOWN AS AVENGERS PRIORITY STATUS.
EXEMPTIONS FROM RESTRICTED AIR TRAFFIC REGULATIONS, ACCESS TO GOVERNMENT DATABASES, EXCLUSIVE COMMUNICATION CHANNELS...
...ALL OF THEM ESSENTIAL FOR US TO DO OUR JOBS EFFECTIVELY.
AND WE DON'T HAVE IT YET.
AT THE MOMENT, WE'RE ON A PROBATIONARY PERIOD, FOR LACK OF A BETTER TERM...
"... NO AVENGER SHALL BE REQUIRED TO SURRENDER KNOWLEDGE OF HIS OR HER CIVILIAN IDENTITY OR PERSONAL AFFAIRS TO THE MEMBERSHIP AT LARGE OR THE NSC..."
WELL, THAT'S PRETTY COOL...
YOU WOULD SAY THAT, YA LITTLE--
THAT'S RIGHT, RICK. PRIVACY IS OF THE UTMOST IMPORTANCE TO PEOPLE IN OUR... PROFESSION.
NOW, YOU'VE ALL GOT COPIES OF THE CHARTER... BUT THIS IS THE ORIGINAL. PRINTED ON SPECIAL PARCHMENT, THERE'S A SPACE AT THE BOTTOM...
...FOR ALL OF US TO SIGN.
OFFICIAL CHARTER
BE IT KNOWN...
That we, the Avengers, have banded together to protect and safeguard the Planet Earth, its inhabitants and resources, from any and all threats -- terrestrial or otherwise -- which are or might prove to be beyond the power of conventional forces to handle.

... WE'RE AVENGERS.
THESE ENVELOPES CONTAIN BOTH OUR CHARTER AND A PROPOSED DRAFT OF OUR BY-LAWS.
I DON'T WANT YOU TO FEEL LIKE I'M HITTING YOU WITH A STACK OF RULES RIGHT OFF THE BAT, BUT BASED ON INITIAL TALKS WITH THE WHITE HOUSE, MR. STARK'S LAWYERS HAVE LAID OUT SPECIFIC POINTS OF INTEREST THAT WE SHOULD DISCUSS AMONG OURSELVES IMMEDIATELY.
"... SAID ORGANIZATION BEING RECOGNIZED AND FULLY SANCTIONED AS A PEACE-KEEPING FORCE BY THE NATIONAL SECURITY COUNCIL..."
THE NSC IS REALLY ONBOARD WITH THIS...?
"...AUTHORIZED TO FUNCTION IN ALL LANDS, TERRITORIES AND PROTECTORATES OF THE U.S...ALL COUNTRIES ALLIED WITH THE U.S. BY INTERNATIONAL TREATY... ALL COUNTRIES AFFILIATED WITH THE UNITED NATIONS..."
LOOKS PRETTY OFFICIAL, HON...
'TIS A LITANY OF NONSENSE TO MINE EYES.
I, FOR ONE, SHALT NOT SUCCUMB TO THE HYPOCRISY OF MIDGARD BUREAUCRACY...
I APPRECIATE YOUR CONCERN, THOR...

I'M SURE WE'RE ALL AWARE OF WHAT'S BEING SAID ABOUT US. THEY'RE SUSPICIOUS, NO DOUBT ABOUT IT.
SUSPICIOUS ABOUT OUR INTENT... SUSPICIOUS ABOUT THIS MEETING... HECK, THEY'RE SUSPICIOUS OF US. WE'LL DEFINITELY HAVE TO WIN THE PUBLIC'S TRUST.
890 Fifth Avenue
890 Fifth Avenue
I'M FAIRLY CERTAIN THAT'LL COME IN TIME...

...BUT IT'LL TAKE EFFORT ON OUR PART. AND IT'S NOT SIMPLY ABOUT GOING OUT AND FIGHTING THE GOOD FIGHT. WE HAVE TO TAKE MEASURES TO ENSURE OUR ABILITY TO OPERATE WITH THE LEAST AMOUNT OF... OUTSIDE INTERFERENCE.
BETWEEN TONY STARK AND MYSELF... WE'VE DONE EVERYTHING WE CAN ON THAT FRONT. I CAN TELL YOU UNEQUIVOCALLY THAT THE SUSPICION I REFERRED TO DOESN'T END WITH THE GENERAL PUBLIC... IT GOES ALL THE WAY UP TO THE HIGHEST LEVELS OF GOVERNMENT. AND BELIEVE ME, THOSE NEGOTIATIONS ARE, SHALL WE SAY, ONGOING...
...LUCKILY, MR. STARK KNOWS HIS WAY AROUND A POLITICO'S OFFICE.

THIS LONG-WINDED PREAMBLE IS MY WAY OF LETTING YOU ALL KNOW HOW SERIOUSLY I'M TAKING THIS. WE'RE DOING SOMETHING MONUMENTAL HERE... SOMETHING THIS UNCERTAIN SOCIETY NEEDS.
I'D ALSO LIKE TO INTRODUCE YOU TO EDWIN JARVIS, SENIOR STAFF MEMBER HERE AT THE MANSION. HE'LL BE PASSING OUT IMPORTANT DOCUMENTS THAT WE NEED TO GO OVER.
FOLKS, WE'VE JUST UPPED THE ANTE IN THE SUPER-POWERED COMMUNITY. WE ARE NO LONGER FIVE DISPARATE HEROES STRUGGLING TO FIND OUR PLACE IN THIS NEW WORLD OF POSSIBILITIES. FROM THIS MOMENT ON...

CRESSKILL, N.J.
WELL, I DOUBT THAT WILL BE REMEMBERED AS OUR FINEST HOUR...
I THINK WE GOT A LOT DONE, HANK. WE SIGNED THE CHARTER, WE TOURED THE MANSION...
SURE.
I THINK I'M GOING TO HEAD INTO THE LAB FOR AWHILE. YOU GO ON TO BED, THOUGH...
TYPICAL WORKAHOLIC.
DARN IT, HANK! WHY DON'T YOU TELL ME WHEN I LOOK THIS AWFUL...!
THAT SKULLCAP WRECKS MY HAIR!
SORRY, JAN. YOU KNOW ME...
...ALWAYS SACRIFICING THE LITTLE DETAILS FOR THE SAKE OF THE BIG PICTURE.

YOU KNOW, SITTING AT THAT MEETING TABLE... LOOKING AROUND AT THE OTHERS...
I DON'T KNOW...I JUST FELT...THEY'RE REAL HEAVYWEIGHTS, JAN...
YOU'RE STILL THE CHAMP TO ME.
FORGET THE LAB FOR TONIGHT. IT'S LATE...
THERE'S GOT TO BE SOMETHING MORE...
THE FORMULA I USE TO GET US BACK TO NORMAL SIZE...IF I CAN TWEAK IT A LITTLE AT THE MOLECULAR LEVEL...
...MAYBE I CAN GET BIGGER THAN THAT.
BIGGER THAN NORMAL? THAT'S THE BEST OPENING FOR A DOUBLE ENTENDRE I'VE HEARD IN MONTHS.
HEY... ARE YOU OKAY...?
PERFECTLY FINE, MISS VAN DYNE.
CHARMER.
NOW TAKE YOUR MEDICINE LIKE A MAN...
YOU MEAN, LIKE A GIANT-MAN...?

STARK INDUSTRIES; TWO WEEKS LATER

AHHH... IT'S YOU.
I WAS EXPECTING YOUR BOSS AT THIS MEETING. AFTER ALL, IT'S HIS HEAD ON THE CHOPPING BLOCK IF THIS ALL GOES SOUTH.

SOMETHING'S DIFFERENT... NEW HAIRSTYLE?
UPGRADES. STANDARD FOR ANY AREA OF TECHNOLOGY.
AND MR. STARK GIVES AN INORDINATE AMOUNT OF TIME TO OUR CAUSE AS IT IS.

WELL, YOU COULD CERTAINLY USE HIM NOW. THIS HULK BUSINESS HAS BECOME A P.R. NIGHTMARE FOR YOU AND YOUR CREW...
YOUR GREEN-SKINNED BOY WENT ON A RAMPAGE IN MIDTOWN MANHATTAN. SCARED THE HELL OUT OF THE LOCALS--

IT... DIDN'T WORK OUT WITH THE HULK, AND HE IS NO LONGER ON OUR ROSTER. WE'RE LOOKING INTO THE RETROACTIVE REMOVAL OF HIS PARTICIPATION IN ALL PERTINENT DOCUMENTS.
NOW, AGENT MURCH... ON THE SUBJECT OF--

SPECIAL AGENT MURCH. LET'S NOT FORGET THAT.
AND LET'S NOT CHANGE THE SUBJECT, EITHER. YOU WENT ON NATIONAL TELEVISION ENDORSING THAT NEANDERTHAL. THE PUBLIC STILL THINKS HE'S YOUR RESPONSIBILITY. SPEAKING FOR THE NATIONAL SECURITY COUNCIL...
...WE'RE NOT HAPPY.

JOIN THE CLUB...
DON'T EXPECT SYMPATHY HERE. YOUR Q-RATING IS IN THE TOILET. YOU THOUGHT IT WAS BAD WHEN YOU ANNOUNCED THIS LITTLE ALLIANCE--
ABOUT THE PRIORITY STATUS...

AHHH... THE BRASS RING.
IF YOU THINK THAT KICKING THE HULK OUT MAKES EVERYTHING ALL RIGHT, YOU'RE SADLY MISTAKEN. I DON'T CARE HOW MANY MUNITIONS DEALS YOUR BOSS HAS CUT WITH THE PENTAGON TO CLEAR YOUR PATH...
...AS LONG AS HE'S RUNNING LOOSE OUT THERE, I WOULDN'T COUNT ON ANY FAVORS FROM THIS OFFICE. ARE WE CLEAR?

I UNDERSTAND, SPECIAL AGENT MURCH. AND I WANT TO ASSURE YOU...
...WE'LL HANDLE IT.

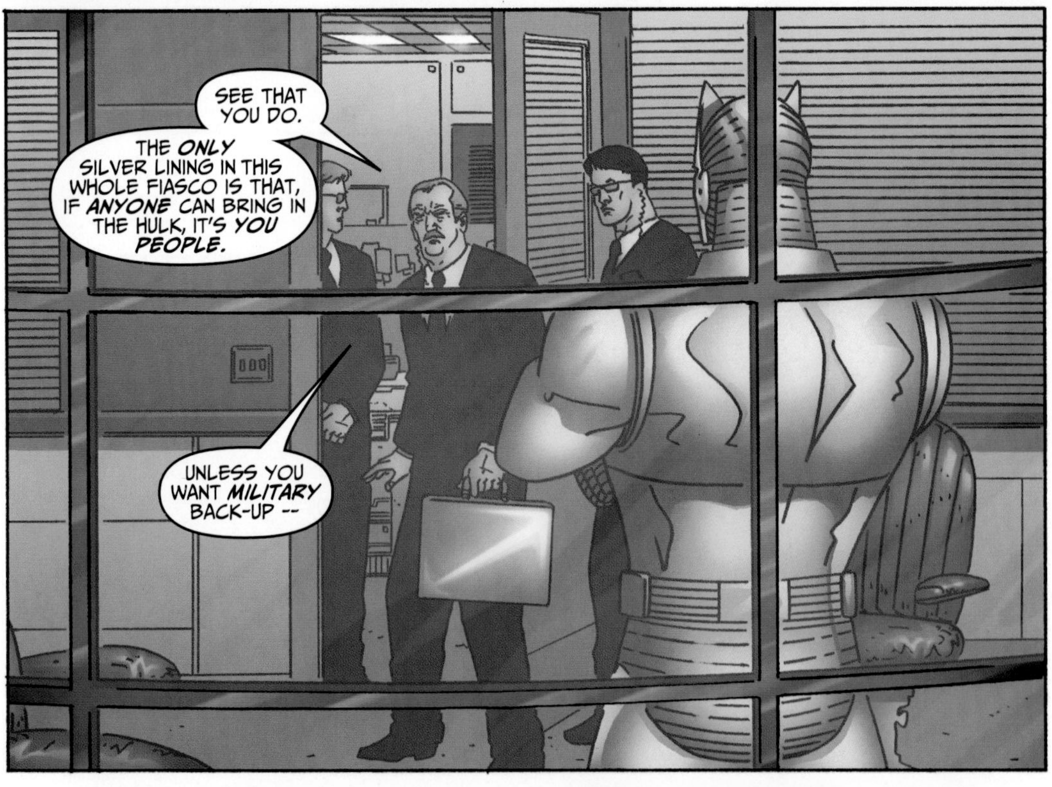
SEE THAT YOU DO.
THE ONLY SILVER LINING IN THIS WHOLE FIASCO IS THAT, IF ANYONE CAN BRING IN THE HULK, IT'S YOU PEOPLE.
UNLESS YOU WANT MILITARY BACK-UP --

I SAID...
...WE'LL HANDLE IT.

--THE HULK IS NOT A MENACE. HIS RECENT PRESIDENTIAL PARDON MERELY REINFORCES OUR POSITION. HE IS ONE OF US.
WE'RE WILLING TO STAKE OUR BURGEONING REPUTATIONS ON HIS VIRTUES AS A HERO...
FURTHERMORE, LET ME SAY--
HEY THERE...
...WE DID THE BEST WE COULD. HE'S...A SAVAGE... THERE WAS HARDLY A MOMENT TO BREATHE--
DON'T PATRONIZE ME--!
WHOA--!
I DON'T NEED YOU TELLING ME --
GIANT-MAN...

...HOLD THY TONGUE.
YOU WILL SHOW RESPECT TO YOUR FELLOW AVENGER. OR ELSE.
SO SPEAKS THOR.

"SO SPEAKS THOR?" WHAT THE DEVIL IS GOING ON BACK HERE...?
IS IT NOT ENOUGH THAT WE GOT TRASHED BY OUR FORMER TEAMMATE? NOW WE'RE HAVING A GO AT EACH OTHER?!

THERE IS NO SHAME WHEN WE HAVE FOUGHT WITH HONOR.
THIS BICKERING IS NOT THE WAY OF WARRIORS FRESH FROM BATTLE.

I SHALL NOT STAND IDLY BY WHILST --
GET OFF YOUR HIGH HORSE, THOR. EVEN I'M ADMITTING WE CAN'T SPIN THIS IN OUR FAVOR!
YOU HAD HIM! AND YOU LET HIM GO! WHAT WERE YOU THINKING?!

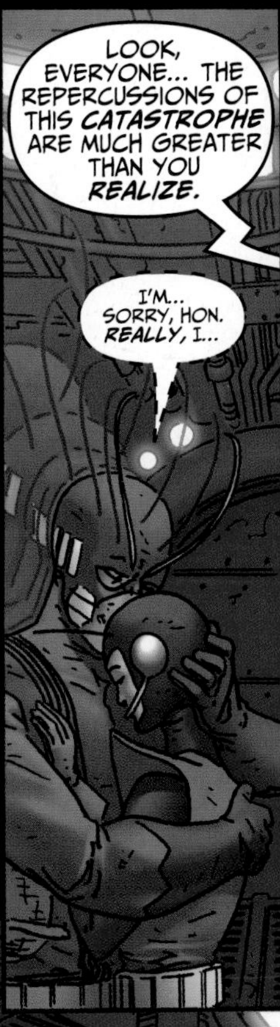
LOOK, EVERYONE... THE REPERCUSSIONS OF THIS CATASTROPHE ARE MUCH GREATER THAN YOU REALIZE.
I'M... SORRY, HON. REALLY, I...

YOU'RE ALL AWARE THAT WE'VE YET TO BE GRANTED OUR PRIORITY STATUS. THERE'S AN AGENT AT THE NSC... MURCH...
...HE'S BEEN ASSIGNED TO US AND IT'S AT HIS DISCRETION WHETHER OR NOT WE GET THAT SECURITY CLEARANCE.
HE'S... USING THIS HULK SITUATION AGAINST US. OUR INABILITY TO CONTAIN HIM WILL NO DOUBT AFFECT MURCH'S DECISION. AT THIS POINT, I DON'T THINK EVEN TONY STARK WILL BE ABLE TO FINAGLE THIS FOR US. IN A WORD...

... WE'RE SCREWED.

THEN... PERHAPS THIS ALLIANCE WAS MADE IN HASTE...
WHAT?!
YOU DIDN'T JUST SAY THAT...! DON'T YOU REALIZE THIS IS TOO IMPORTANT TO GIVE UP ON NOW?!
I MEAN, WHAT KIND OF "GOD" ARE YOU?!
DO NOT TEST ME, WOMAN --
DON'T EVEN THINK ABOUT IT, THOR. SHE'S RIGHT AND YOU KNOW IT. TRY USING YOUR HEAD FOR A MINUTE --
THY TONE IS INSULTING.
I DO NOT ALLOW SUCH DISRESPECT.
IS THAT A FACT? Y'KNOW, THAT HAMMER DOESN'T GIVE YOU THE RIGHT TO LORD YOURSELF OVER ANYONE IN HERE!
UNLESS YOU PLAN ON USING THAT THING ON ME NOW...

I...
...WILL NOT FIGHT YOU.

THANK GOD.
LOOK... MAYBE I CAN RIG A GAMMA TRACER TO GET A BEAD ON THE HULK'S MOVEMENTS BEFORE THE REST OF YOU HAVE SOME KIND OF MELTDOWN--

HEY, JUST BECAUSE YOU AND YOUR BOSS ARE LETTING THE NSC RUN ROUGHSHOD OVER YOUR BLOATED EGOS--
BACK OFF, ANT--I MEAN-- GIANT-MAN!
JUST WHO THE HELL DO YOU THINK YOU--

BREEP! BREEP! BREEP!

THAT ALARM... THE SONAR NET...
IS... SOMETHING OUT THERE...?
WHAT THE--?!
PORT SIDE... AHEAD ONE HUNDRED METERS...
IT'S NOT MARINE LIFE. SPECTRAL ANALYSIS IS PICKING UP...

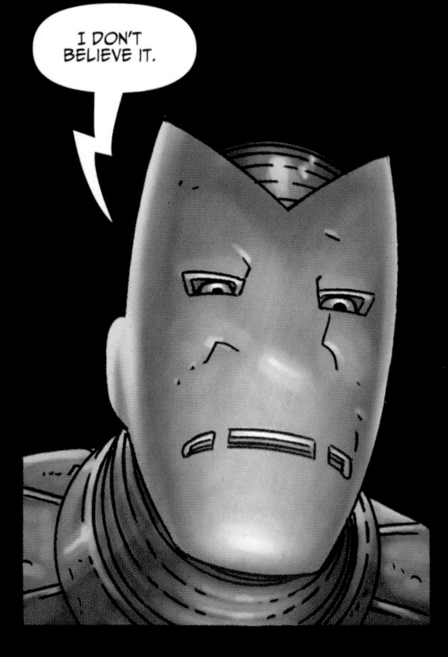
I DON'T BELIEVE IT.

#2
KOLINS 04

...TRACES OF VITA-RAY BOMBARDMENT CONSISTENT WITH THE FEW NOTES EXISTING ON OPERATION: REBIRTH.
BUT WHAT'S MOST FASCINATING IS ITS EFFECT WHILE FROZEN IN THE ICE. THE FORMULA ACTUALLY PREVENTED CRYSTALLIZATION OF HIS BODILY FLUIDS...
...WHICH EXPLAINS THE SURVIVABLE STATE OF SUSPENDED ANIMATION WE FOUND HIM IN.
SOME PECULIAR BRAIN ACTIVITY, THOUGH. I SUPPOSE I'LL HAVE TO RUN MORE TESTS...
END VOICE LOG
OKAY, WE'RE DONE FOR NOW. SORRY IT TOOK SO LONG.
HOW'RE YOU DOING IN HERE...?

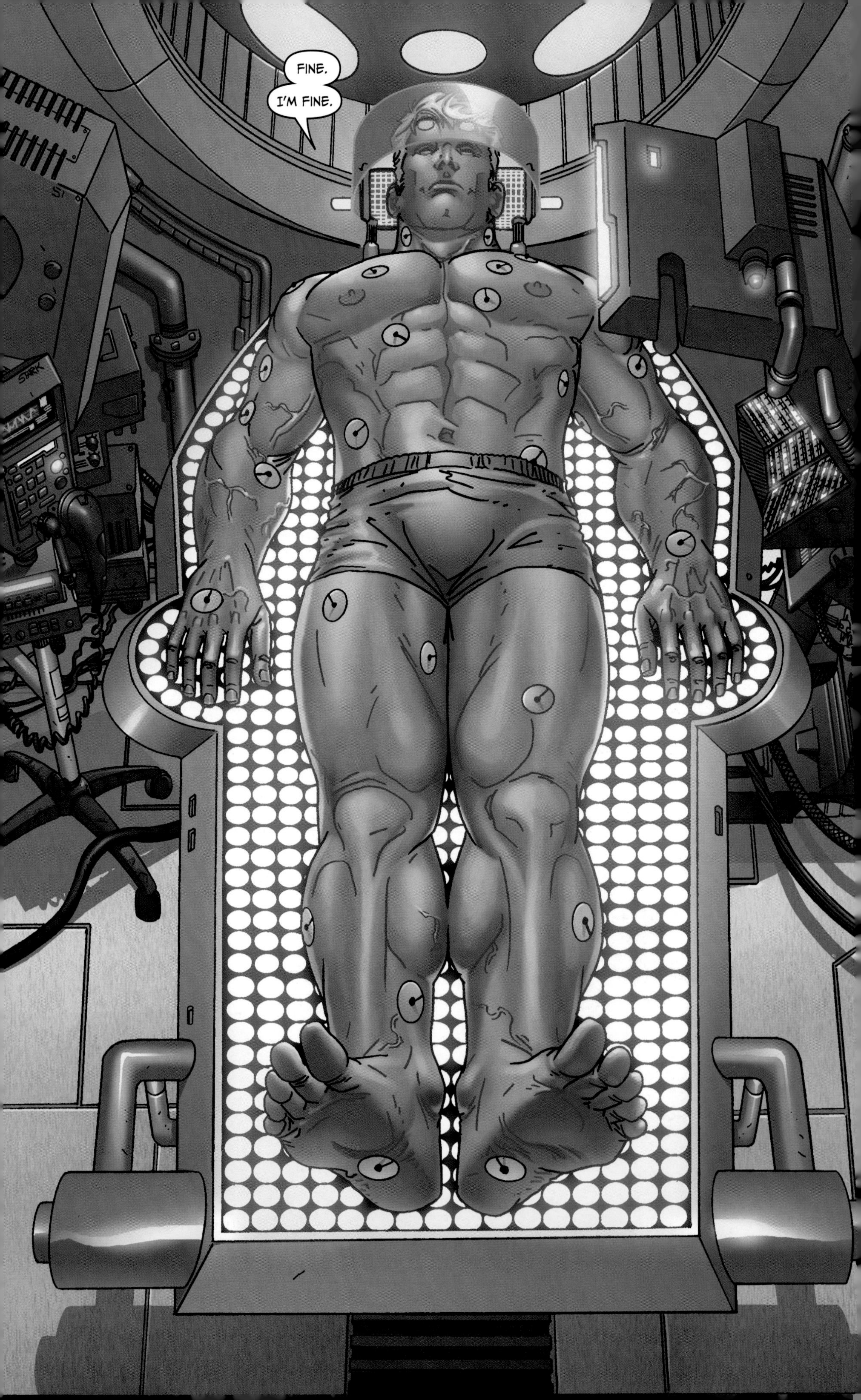
FINE.
I'M FINE.
STARK

WE MAY DO SOME FOLLOW-UP TESTS AT SOME POINT, BUT I DON'T WANT TO KEEP YOU LOCKED UP IN HERE ALL DAY.
I'LL BET YOU'RE FREEZING. HERE...
TELL YOU THE TRUTH, I HAVEN'T GOTTEN WARM SINCE... WELL...
WELL, I CAN... IMAGINE.
I GUESS I SHOULD JUST SHUT UP AND BE GRATEFUL.
IS THE EXAMINATION COMPLETE? MAY I ENTER...?
SURE. C'MON IN, JARVIS.
I'VE BROUGHT COFFEE.
PERFECT TIMING. YOU MUST HAVE A SIXTH SENSE ABOUT THESE THINGS.
YOU'VE MET CAPTAIN AMERICA...?
YES, WELL...
...JUST BRIEFLY... BEFORE...
YOU'RE STARING, JARVIS.

NOT THAT I BLAME YOU. THIS IS A BONA FIDE LIVING LEGEND STANDING IN OUR MIDST.
I MEAN, I'VE READ AT LEAST TWENTY BOOKS ABOUT YOU.
MAYBE I SHOULD READ THEM. IT MIGHT HELP WITH THESE MEMORY GAPS...
I'M SURE IT'LL ALL COME BACK IN TIME.
JARVIS, YOU SHOULD'VE SEEN THE LOOKS ON OUR FACES WHEN WE PULLED THAT HUNK OF ICE IN FROM THE OCEAN. SENSORS HAD PICKED UP A HUMAN BIO-SIGNATURE...
...BUT ONCE WE SAW THE UNIFORM... THE WASP ALMOST HAD A HEART ATTACK.
IT WAS DEFINITELY A MOMENT FOR THE HISTORY BOOKS...
I KNOW I GOT A LITTLE CRAZY WHEN I CAME TO, GIANT-MAN... I HOPE I DIDN'T HURT ANYONE...
...I JUST... DIDN'T KNOW WHERE I WAS... I COULDN'T...
MY GOD.
MAYBE YOU SHOULD TAKE HIM BACK TO HIS ROOM. I NEED TO COLLATE THE DATA I'VE GATHERED AND SPEAK TO THE OTHERS.
OF COURSE.

IF YOU'LL COME THIS WAY, SIR...
YOU LEAD, I'LL FOLLOW.
OH, AND IF I HAVEN'T SAID THIS ALREADY... THANK YOU.
MY PLEASURE, CAPTAIN.
CALL ME STEVE.
...I'VE STOCKED MORE CLEAN CLOTHES. STARK INDUSTRIES ISSUE, I'M AFRAID. THERE'S THE TELEVISION... FRESH TOWELS ARE IN THE BATHROOM...
...THE PAPERS ON THE TABLE... THEY'RE FROM THE PENTAGON. SOMETHING ABOUT BACK PAY...
UHHH... THANKS.
YOUR... UNIFORM IS HANGING IN THE CLOSET. MISTER STARK HAD IT FULLY RESTORED.
IN ANY CASE... SLEEP WELL, SIR. YOU'VE CERTAINLY EARNED IT.

Welcome back, Cap.
Tony Stark

TELEVISION...

KLK
--YOU GOTTA BEAT HER TIME AND EAT THE MOST MAGGOTS...

READY... GO!

DON'T PUKE, GAIL! DON'T PUKE! YOU CAN DO IT--

KLK
--CONTINUING TENSIONS IN THE MIDDLE EAST, AS U.N. TROOPS WERE AMBUSHED BY LOCAL MILITIA FORCES. RETALIATION WAS SWIFT AND--
AQABA

KLK
...SO THEN YOU TELL ME, GOVERNOR! CAN YOU GET THROUGH A FISCAL QUARTER WITHOUT HARASSING YOUR FEMALE PAGES IN THE CAPITOL BUILDING--?!
KLK
--AND GOD IS DEAD...AND SO IS YOUR MOOOOMMM--!
--GO AHEAD AND SETCHA SCHOOL ON FIIIIRREEE--
KLK

...SO PHYSICALLY, HE'S WELL ON HIS WAY TO A COMPLETE RECOVERY.
THAT SERUM THEY GAVE HIM... ITS EFFECT ON HIS PHYSIOLOGY REMAINS UNDIMINISHED, EVEN AFTER ALL THESE YEARS.
WELL, DR. ERSKINE WAS AT THE VERY TOP OF HIS FIELD...UNTIL HE WAS ASSASSINATED.
AS FOR OUR NEWFOUND FRIEND, HE HASN'T BEEN SEEN SINCE 1945. ARMY INTEL LISTS HIM AS M.I.A. THAT COULD MEAN ANYTHING.
SO, ARE WE ALL CONVINCED... THIS IS THE REAL CAPTAIN AMERICA...?
THESE ARE HIS ARMY RECORDS, IN FULL. PHYSICAL EXAMS, BLOOD WORK, PSYCHOLOGICAL TESTING...STATE OF THE ART FOR THE ERA. MY DATA PERFECTLY MATCHES THESE SPECS. SO IT'S DEFINITELY HIM. BUT THERE'S SOMETHING ELSE...
AT THIS POINT, I'M A LITTLE SKEPTICAL ABOUT HIS CAPACITY TO FUNCTION EMOTIONALLY. HE'S STILL COPING WITH THE REALITY OF HIS SITUATION. FOR HIM TO CONSIDER ACTIVE DUTY AGAIN...IT COULD BE PROBLEMATIC ON SEVERAL LEVELS.
ANYWAY, THAT'S MY PERSPECTIVE.
LET IT BE SAID... I HAVE KNOWN WARRIORS WRONGLY BANISHED TO NIFFLEHEIM ITSELF WHO HAVE RETURNED TO PERFORM EVEN GREATER GLORIES...
"NIFFLEHEIM".
I SEE.
OKAY, LET'S NOT GET INTO A FULL-ON DEBATE ABOUT THIS JUST YET. LET'S GIVE HIM SOME TIME TO ADJUST. THEN WE'LL SEE WHERE WE ARE.
IN THE MEANTIME, THERE'S A BIT MORE RESEARCH TO BE DONE. SOMETHING I'D LIKE TO CHECK INTO...

A-HA!
I WAS RIGHT!
THIS IS FANTASTIC!
I TAKE IT YOU'VE FOUND SOMETHING OF INTEREST...?
THAT'S PUTTING IT MILDLY, THOR.
CAP'S STATUS AS AN ARMY SPECIAL OPERATIVE AUTOMATICALLY GRANTS HIM THE KIND OF ACROSS-THE-BOARD SECURITY CLEARANCE WE'VE BEEN FIGHTING TO GET.
HERE'S THE THING... THERE'S A LOOPHOLE. IT APPLIES TO ANY OF CAP'S WARTIME ALLIES UNDER A "PROVISIONAL SECURITY CLEARANCE" CLAUSE. WE CAN USE THAT.
YOUR INTENTIONS ARE ADMIRABLE. BUT ANY ACHIEVEMENT ON THE BASIS OF A CONTRACTUAL TECHNICALITY...
...THERE IS VERY LITTLE HONOR IN THAT.
I'M SORRY YOU FEEL THAT WAY. I WISH WE HAD A MORE "HONORABLE" ALTERNATIVE.
IF WE CAN PROVE OURSELVES TO THE N.S.C. QUICKLY, I DON'T SEE HOW THEY WON'T--
I DO NOT LIVE IN A WORLD WHERE I MUST "PROVE MYSELF" TO POLITICIANS...
WE DON'T ALL LIVE IN YOUR WORLD, THOR.
BUT I'LL DO WHATEVER IT TAKES TO MAKE SURE EVERYTHING WE'VE BUILT HERE DOESN'T GO TO POT. IF YOU DON'T AGREE WITH MY LEADERSHIP CHOICES, DON'T HOLD BACK.
I'M LISTENING.

YOUR... "LEADERSHIP"...
PERHAPS THOU ART LABORING UNDER FALSE PRESUMPTIONS, IRON MAN. OUR INTERNAL STRUGGLES PALE IN COMPARISON TO OUR TRUE GOALS... TO SOUNDLY SMITE THE ENEMIES OF MORTAL MAN. TO AVENGE THOSE WHO HAVE SUFFERED THE EVIL OF THIS WORLD.
YOU WOULD DO WELL NOT TO CONFUSE THOSE OBJECTIVES WITH YOUR PERSONAL CRUSADES...
...
RIGHT.
IF YOU'RE TRYING TO KEEP ME ON MY TOES... YOU'RE DOING A GOOD JOB.
I'D PROPOSE A TEMPORARY DETENTE... BUT I DOUBT IT'S IN YOUR NATURE.
AND I'M SURE THAT WHERE YOU COME FROM--WHEREVER THAT MIGHT BE--YOU DON'T HAVE TO DEAL WITH ALL THE RED TAPE THAT, QUITE HONESTLY, MAKES ME WANT TO STRANGLE SOMEONE...
...BUT I'M IN TOO DEEP NOW. I'M TOO COMMITTED TO SEE THIS FAIL.
SO...
...IF I ASK YOU ABOUT ASGARD, WILL I GET ANOTHER FLOWERY SPEECH--
--OR ARE YOU FINALLY GOING TO LEVEL WITH ME?
I MEAN, YOU CLAIM GODHOOD... BUT I'M JUST NOT SURE IF I CAN...
THOR...?
SIGH
I HATE IT WHEN HE DOES THAT...!

NO!

PANT
PANT
PANT
AHHHH...
...HELLO...?
OH.
HEY.
HOW'S IT GOING...?

DON'T MIND **ME.** JUST... Y'KNOW... RAIDING THE FRIDGE. JARVIS MAKES A MEAN EGG SALAD...
OH, WHERE'S **MY** MANNERS, HUH?
RICK JONES. NICE T'MEET YOU.
STEVE... ROGERS...
UNBELIEVABLE...!
UHHH... YOU OKAY...?
I'M FINE. JUST... COULDN'T SLEEP...
SO YOU'RE NOT A **PROWLER.** THEN, WHO **ARE** YOU...? I MEAN--
YOU MEAN, WHO AM I TO THE **AVENGERS?** *PUH-LEEZE--!*
IF IT WASN'T FOR **ME,** THESE GUYS NEVER WOULD'VE GOT TOGETHER IN THE **FIRST** PLACE!
A... UHHH... **FRIEND** OF MINE GOT IN A LITTLE **TROUBLE.** I CALLED FOR SOME **HELP.** THEY ANSWERED. AFTERWARDS, THEY DECIDED THAT A **VARSITY TEAM** MIGHT NOT BE SUCH A BAD IDEA--
I'M AFRAID I CAN'T SAY THE SAME OF MY DECISION TO GIVE YOU A **KEY,** MISTER JONES.
THESE LATE NIGHT VISITS ARE BEGINNING TO RATTLE MY **NERVES.**
SHALL I MAKE A FRESH POT OF COFFEE...?

...SO I DO WHAT I CAN TO KEEP THE BIG GREEN LUG IN LINE. AND LEMME TELL YOU...IT'S STEADY WORK.
COULDN'T KEEP HIM AROUND HERE, BUT WHATEVER. SOME THINGS AREN'T MEANT TO BE. HE'S KEPT THESE GUYS BUSY, THAT'S FOR SURE...
BET YOU'VE BEEN IN A FEW HAIRY SITUATIONS, HUH? LIKE, BEHIND ENEMY LINES AN' ALL THAT...
WELL... I DON'T...
PLEASE FORGIVE HIM, SIR...
...HE MAY BE A BIT TOO YOUNG TO REALIZE THAT MEMORIES OF WAR ARE NEVER PLEASANT ONES.
I... HESITATE TO SAY THIS, SIR. WHAT YOU MEANT TO THAT GENERATION... AND SUBSEQUENT GENERATIONS THAT NEEDED YOU MORE THAN YOU'LL EVER KNOW...
...YOU WERE MORE THAN A SOLDIER. YOU WERE A SYMBOL OF EVERY DECENT THING THIS COUNTRY HAS EVER FOUGHT FOR.
TO THINK THAT YOU COULD BE THAT AGAIN...
NO PRESSURE, JARV! GEEZ...
OF COURSE... YOU'RE RIGHT...
MY APOLOGIES, SIR. IT'S...NOT MY PLACE TO SAY SUCH THINGS.

IT'S OKAY, JARVIS. AND I HONESTLY DON'T MIND THE QUESTIONS...
I JUST...
...CAN'T REMEMBER MUCH.
NO WORRIES, CAP. YOU GOT ENOUGH TO DEAL WITH JUST MEMORIZING THE CABLE STATIONS...
UH-OH...MY WATCH SAYS IT'S TIME TO HIT IT. GOT A DAY AHEAD OF ME...
THANKS FOR THE GRUB, JARVIS. FREE FOOD'S A HELLUVA PERK IN THIS BUSINESS.
HANG IN THERE, CAP. YOU'LL BE BACK TO BUTT-KICKING AND NAME-TAKING IN NO TIME.
ADIOS, AMIGOS!
KID'S A HANDFUL, EH...?
SIR, YOU HAVE NO IDEA...

...WHAT CAN YOU TELL ME ABOUT THESE "AVENGERS"? WHAT ARE THEY TRYING TO DO HERE...?
AHH, YES. A LEGITIMATE QUERY...
HONEST, THEY'VE BEEN TRYING TO FIGURE THAT OUT THEMSELVES.
IT'S NOT AN EASY THING THEY'RE ATTEMPTING...FORMING AN ALLIANCE WHOSE SOLE PURPOSE IS TO PROTECT THE INNOCENT FROM WHATEVER THREATS MAY ARISE.
I'M SURE IT'S THEIR HOPE THAT YOU'LL JOIN THEM IN THEIR MISSION...
ME...?
LOOK, JARVIS... I CAN'T FAULT THEIR INTENTIONS...
...BUT I DON'T KNOW IF THAT'S THE RIGHT CHOICE FOR ME.
BELONG HERE. IN THIS TIME PERIOD. IT'S A FLUKE THAT I'M EVEN ALIVE...!
THE WORLD HAS CHANGED SO DRASTICALLY...I MIGHT END UP BEING MORE OF A HINDRANCE THAN A HELP TO THEM...
I'D LIKE TO SHOW YOU SOMETHING...
...IN THE STUDY.
LOOKS LIKE NO ONE COMES IN HERE...
NO ONE DOES. CURRENTLY, YOU ARE THE MANSION'S ONLY RESIDENT.
BESIDES ME, OF COURSE.
AND YOU'RE CORRECT. THIS IS A MUCH DIFFERENT ERA THAN THE ONE YOU CAME FROM. I SEE PEOPLE HAVING TROUBLE FINDING SOMETHING TO BELIEVE IN...
YOU HAVE RETURNED TO A WORLD STARVING FOR INSPIRATION. WHETHER THEY KNOW IT OR NOT, THE AVENGERS HAVE THE ABILITY TO PROVIDE THAT. BUT DON'T TAKE MY WORD FOR IT...
...I THINK THIS STATES THEIR PUPOSE--AND THEIR POTENTIAL--MUCH BETTER THAN I EVER COULD.
I'VE FOUND SOMETHING THAT I BELIEVE IN.
ONCE YOU READ THAT...PERHAPS YOU WILL, TOO.
OFFICIAL CHARTER
BE IT KNOWN,

ONE WEEK LATER

AVENGERS! WE NEED A BARRICADE!

WHOA--!
I GOT ONE RIGHT ON MY--

GAH--!
HEY... THANKS, CAP. I--
YOU SHOULDN'T BE HERE!

I DON'T KNOW HOW LONG I CAN HOLD THEM BACK!
MY TRANSISTORS--
I'M HERE, IRON MAN--!
MIGHT BE TOO LITTLE, TOO LATE! THE ROCK'S GONE MOLTEN! WON'T BE LONG BEFORE--
STEP ASIDE, GENTLEMEN...
...I'VE GOT THIS ONE.

NOT BAD, PEOPLE. A LITTLE TEAM-WORK GOES A LONG WAY...
I DID A QUICK RECON. FOR THE MOMENT, THEY'VE CLEARED OUT...
WHERE ON EARTH IS THOR...?!
SPEAK OF THE DEVIL.
THE NEGOTIATIONS WENT WELL. THESE CREATURES SHALL FOREVER REMAIN IN THEIR SUBTERRANEAN DOMAIN.
THEY WILL NOT SOON FORGET THAT THE AVENGERS GUARD THE GATES OF MORTAL CIVILIZATION...
HEADS UP, PARTNERS. THE ARMY'S MOVING IN.
FRANKLY, I'M STILL SHOCKED THEY COMPLIED WITH OUR REQUEST THAT THEY STAND DOWN...
WHEN CAPTAIN AMERICA'S ASKING, WHO'S GOING TO REFUSE HIM? RIGHT, CAP...?
CAP...?

...PERHAPS THE MOST SIGNIFICANT DEVELOPMENT IN THE RECENT EMERGENCE OF AMERICAN SUPER HEROES IS THE RETURN OF THE ORIGINAL SUPER HERO, CAPTAIN AMERICA. OUR NEWS TEAM HIT THE STREETS TO ASK NEW YORKERS THEIR OPINIONS...
RETURN OF A LEGEND?

I COULDN'T BELIEVE IT WHEN I HEARD! I MEAN... THE STORIES MY GRANDFATHER TOLD ME ABOUT HIM...!
WHAT CAN I SAY? GIVES ME HOPE...

"HOPE"...
...COULDN'T HAVE PUT IT BETTER MYSELF, AGENT MURCH...
BUT NOT EVERYONE IS SO EASILY CONVINCED BY THE NEWS OF CAPTAIN AMERICA'S RETURN...
I DUNNO... HOW DO WE KNOW HE'S THE REAL THING?
FOR ALL I KNOW, HE COULD BE SOME RINGER IN A FLAG COSTUME...!

OH, GOOD LORD...!
IT NEVER FAILS. THE CYNICISM OF MODERN SOCIETY...
WELL, YOU SEEMED FINE ABOUT THE GUY BURSTING WITH HOPE...
PEOPLE AREN'T GOING TO FALL ALL OVER THEMSELVES JUST BECAUSE YOUR FRIENDS ARE HANGING OUT WITH A WAR HERO...EVEN IF IT IS CAPTAIN AMERICA.

YOU KNOW HE'S THE REAL DEAL.

THE CAPTAIN'S PRIORITY STATUS TO FLY INTO RESTRICTED AIRSPACE...
YOU CAN LET THEM KNOW FROM ME... THEY WON'T BE USING HIM AS AN EXCUSE AGAIN.

MURCH...
...AND I KNOW FOR A FACT THAT THE ARMY WAS GRATEFUL FOR THE ASSISTANCE.

MAYBE THEY WERE. BUT THE N.S.C. DOESN'T APPRECIATE WHEN PEOPLE DON'T TAKE US SERIOUSLY.
AND THE BIG DEAL THEY'VE MADE ABOUT CAPTAIN AMERICA IN THEIR RANKS... WE'RE NOT COMPLETELY CONVINCED HE'S MENTALLY FIT FOR THE JOB.

THE MAN'S BEEN ON ICE FOR DECADES, STARK! CAN YOU IMAGINE WHAT THAT'S DONE FOR HIS HEAD...?!

HAVE YOU TALKED TO HIM?
NOT YET...

...BUT I'VE READ EVERYTHING ON HIS RETURN. HIS REINTEGRATION INTERVIEWS, HIS LENGTHY DEBRIEFINGS... THE MAN DOESN'T EVEN REMEMBER HOW HE GOT HERE!

OKAY...LET'S TRY A DIFFERENT TACK...
LET'S SAY HE CHECKS OUT...TO YOUR SATISFACTION...
...WOULD THAT ENSURE THE AVENGERS THEIR SECURITY CLEARANCE?
HE IS A NATIONAL HERO. AN ICON...
STARK, I HAVE TO TELL YOU...
...IT'S SO MUCH EASIER TO TALK DIRECTLY TO YOU. IT'S CERTAINLY MORE PRODUCTIVE THAN DEALING WITH A BODYGUARD WITH DELUSIONS OF GRANDEUR...
I TRUST IRON MAN WITH MY LIFE.
AS FOR CAPTAIN AMERICA--
FINE. JUST BETWEEN US...
...YOUR FRIENDS' CHANCES HAVE CERTAINLY IMPROVED WITH THE GOOD CAPTAIN ON THEIR SIDE. MY BOSSES CAN BE SUCKERS FOR THAT PATRIOTIC CRAP.
CAN I QUOTE YOU ON THAT...?
I'M A TRUE PATRIOT, STARK.
THAT MEANS...I'M GOING TO BE WATCHING THE AVENGERS VERY CLOSELY. IT'S POSSIBLE THIS COULD WORK OUT FOR THEM...AND FOR CAPTAIN AMERICA...
...IF HE DOESN'T CRACK UNDER THE PRESSURE, THAT IS.

#3

...NEAR THE TULAROSA BASIN IN NEW MEXICO, ANOTHER INTENSE CONFRONTATION BETWEEN **U.S. MILITARY FORCES** AND THE CREATURE KNOWN ONLY AS THE **HULK.**
DESERT RAMPAGE
SEVERAL REPORTED **CASUALTIES** RELATED TO THIS CONFLICT ONLY ADD TO THE LIST OF **CHARGES** LEVELED AGAINST THE CREATURE...
MY GOD...
...IT'S JUST GETTING **WORSE,** ISN'T IT...?

I MEAN, THEY'RE GOING TO END UP **KILLING** HIM, AREN'T THEY...?
I...*UHHH*... COULDN'T SAY, JAN.
PERSONALLY, I THINK HE'S TOO MUCH FOR THE **ARMY** TO HANDLE...
Y'KNOW, I THINK I'LL HEAD INTO THE **LAB** FOR AWHILE.
YOU'LL... *UMMM*...BE OKAY IN HERE, WATCHING THE NEWS CHANNELS, RIGHT...?
ALRIGHT, THEN...
C'MON, CORPORAL...THE AMERICAN PEOPLE DESERVE TO KNOW HOW **FAR** YOU GUYS'LL GO TO BRING THIS BEAST **DOWN.**
FOR EXAMPLE, ARE YOU PREPARED TO USE **NUCLEAR** WEAPONS ON AMERICAN SOIL...?

HEY THERE, HIGH-POCKETS.
YOU THINK IT'S THAT EASY? YOU THINK YOU CAN JUST SHUFFLE OUT OF A ROOM LIKE THAT...?

WHAT'S THE MATTER, HANK?
NOTHING.
I JUST...HAD A FEW THOUGHTS ON PERFECTING THE GROWTH FORMULA. I THINK I CAN REDUCE THE STRAIN ON OUR BODIES IF I JUST--

HANK.
I'M NOT BUYING IT.
LOOK...WE'RE NOT MUTANTS. WE DON'T WEAR ARMOR. WE'RE NOT GODS. OUR ABILITIES ARE SCIENTIFIC. THAT MEANS THEIR LIMITATIONS...ARE MY LIMITATIONS.
I KNOW I CAN DO BETTER. I JUST... NEED A LITTLE TIME. SOME PEACE AND QUIET...

OKAY.
I HEAR YOU.

...WITH THE HULK STILL AT LARGE, THERE IS A FUNDAMENTAL QUESTION ON THE MINDS OF THE AMERICAN PEOPLE...

...WHERE ARE THE AVENGERS? CONSIDERING THEIR VERY PUBLIC STATEMENTS ON THE HULK AT THEIR INCEPTION...

...AND TAKING INTO ACCOUNT THEIR EXPRESSED INTENT TO DEAL WITH THREATS OF THIS EXACT NATURE, I THINK WE ALL NEED TO FACE CERTAIN HARD TRUTHS ABOUT THEIR ORGANIZATION.
FROM MY PERSPECTIVE, THIS IS A MYSTERIOUS AND SCARY GROUP OF INDIVIDUALS.
THE FACT THAT THEY STOOD UP FOR THE HULK IN THE FIRST PLACE MAKES THEM SUSPECT!
I KNOW I WOULDN'T CALL THEM IF MY CAT WAS STUCK IN A TREE!
BZZZT
YES...?
JUST WANTED TO LET YOU KNOW BEFORE I LEFT FOR THE DAY...SPECIAL AGENT MURCH CALLED. HE'S REQUESTING A MEETING WITH IRON MAN AS SOON AS POSSIBLE.
FINE. I'LL LET HIM KNOW.
GOOD NIGHT, PEPPER.
...SHOULD WE STILL CONSIDER THE HULK TO BE THEIR ALLY? AND, IF HE'S NOT, WHY HAVEN'T THEY BROUGHT HIM TO JUSTICE?
IS THE HULK'S BEHAVIOR MERELY INDICATIVE OF THE QUESTIONABLE NATURE OF THIS GROUP?
THEY SAY THEY'RE HEROES. SHOULD WE BELIEVE THEM...?

MORE COFFEE, GENTLEMEN?
OH, ARE YOU KIDDING? A MAN CAN'T GET TOO MUCH CAFFEINE IN HIS SYSTEM. BRING IT ON...!
I THINK YOU'VE HAD QUITE ENOUGH, MISTER JONES.
WHATEVER.
Y'KNOW, THESE OP-ED PIECES... THEY CAN'T STOP TALKING ABOUT YOU, CAP.
YOU'VE BECOME A REGULAR URBAN LEGEND. THERE'S SIGHTINGS OF YOU ALL OVER NOW. HERE'S ONE FROM A SHOPPING MALL IN OHIO...
SIR...YOUR BREAKFAST...
I'M...SORRY, JARVIS. I GUESS I'M JUST NOT HUNGRY.
HEY, CAP...YOU WANT THIS? CATCH UP ON CURRENT EVENTS AN' ALL THAT JAZZ?
NOT RIGHT NOW, RICK...
...NOT RIGHT NOW.

WELL...
...IF YOU'LL EXCUSE ME...
HEY, JARVIS...!
WHAT'S THE MATTER WITH HIM? HE'S, LIKE... OUT TO LUNCH, BIG-TIME...
WELL, TRY PLACING YOURSELF IN HIS SHOES. HIS ACCLIMATION INTO MODERN SOCIETY WON'T BE ACHIEVED BY MERELY READING THE NEWSPAPER...!
SIGH

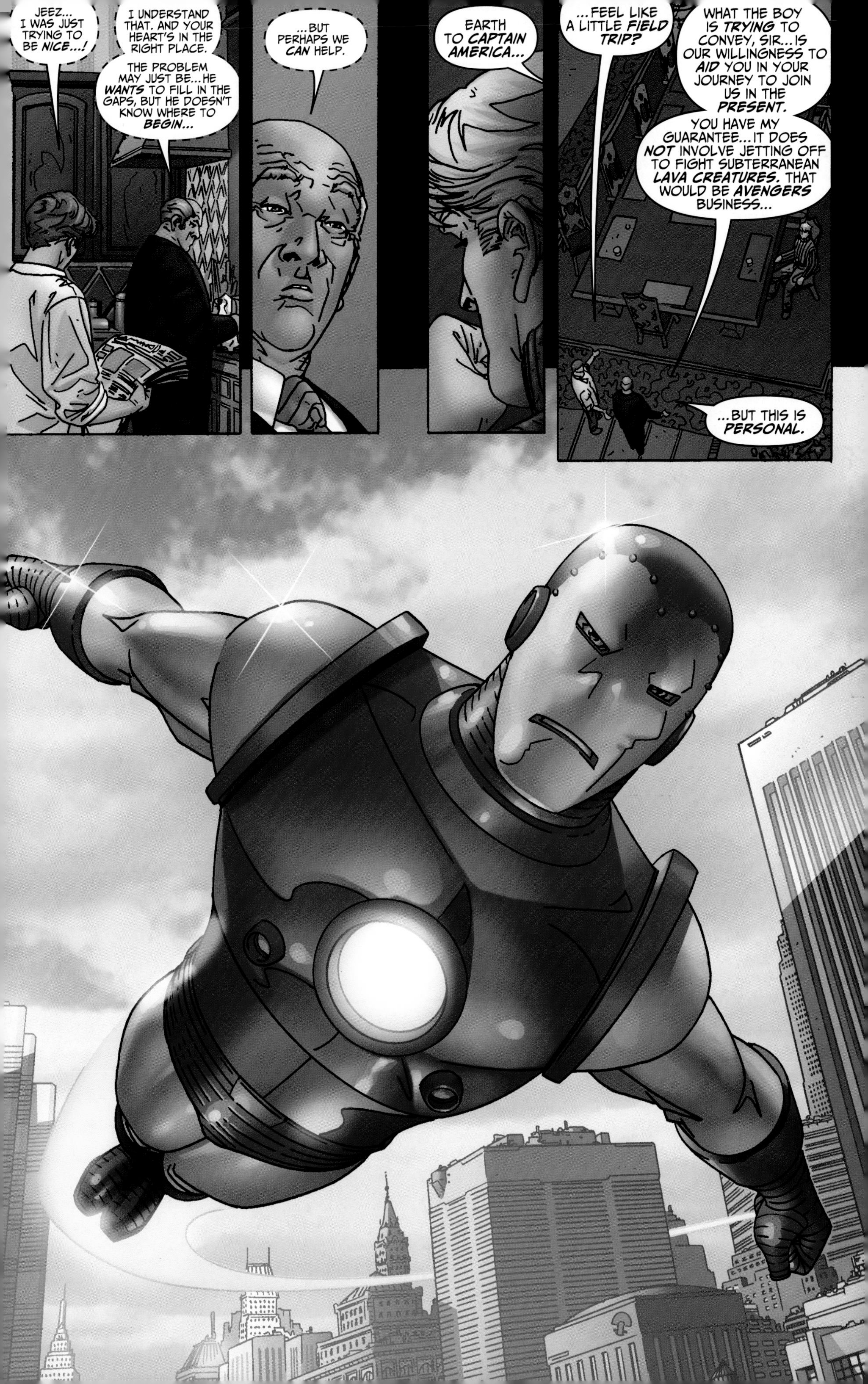
JEEZ... I WAS JUST TRYING TO BE NICE...!
I UNDERSTAND THAT. AND YOUR HEART'S IN THE RIGHT PLACE.
THE PROBLEM MAY JUST BE...HE WANTS TO FILL IN THE GAPS, BUT HE DOESN'T KNOW WHERE TO BEGIN...
...BUT PERHAPS WE CAN HELP.
EARTH TO CAPTAIN AMERICA...
...FEEL LIKE A LITTLE FIELD TRIP?
WHAT THE BOY IS TRYING TO CONVEY, SIR...IS OUR WILLINGNESS TO AID YOU IN YOUR JOURNEY TO JOIN US IN THE PRESENT.
YOU HAVE MY GUARANTEE...IT DOES NOT INVOLVE JETTING OFF TO FIGHT SUBTERRANEAN LAVA CREATURES. THAT WOULD BE AVENGERS BUSINESS...
...BUT THIS IS PERSONAL.

YOU'RE TWO MINUTES LATE, IRON MAN.
MAYBE YOU WERE TWO MINUTES EARLY, AGENT MURCH...
COULD BE. I DO LOVE MY JOB.
NICE HANGAR DOOR. I ASSUME YOU'VE CLEARED THE BUILDING CODES WITH OUR OFFICE IN WASHINGTON. IN ANY CASE...
...THIS MAN IS THE REASON I CALLED THIS MEETING. GENERAL PAUL WALLACE, VICE-CHAIRMAN OF THE JOINT CHIEFS OF STAFF.
WHAT IS THIS... A SETUP?
HARDLY.
YOU'RE OBVIOUSLY FORGETTING THAT I DON'T NEED TO BE SNEAKY TO MAKE YOU FOLKS LOOK BAD.
YOU'RE UP, GENERAL...
NO DOUBT YOU'RE AWARE THAT YOUR EMPLOYER HAS CUT SEVERAL DEALS WITH US ON WEAPONS CONTRACTS TO MASSAGE YOUR RELATIONSHIP WITH THE DEFENSE COMMUNITY. THE PRIVATE SECTOR...THAT'S ANOTHER STORY. HOWEVER...
...WE'RE HERE TO MAKE YOU A DEAL NOW.
HOW WOULD THE AVENGERS RESPOND TO BEING AN OFFICIAL BRANCH OF THE MILITARY...?

AN OFFICIAL... WHAT...?!
TECHNICALLY, YOU'D BE OPERATING AS A SUPER-POWERED SPECIAL FORCES DIVISION...
...ORGANIZED EMPLOYMENT OF A PARAMILITARY UNIT IN SUSTAINED COMBAT AGAINST A DETERMINED ENEMY.

IT'S JUST A PROTOTYPE, MURCH...
GENERAL... JUST WHAT KIND OF AUTHORITY WOULD THE PENTAGON HAVE OVER US?
SOUNDS LIKE A NO-BRAINER, IF YOU ASK ME. YOU'D CERTAINLY BE GRANTED AUTOMATIC A-1 PRIORITY CLEARANCE...
...WHICH, I SHOULD ADD, YOU'VE YET TO ACHIEVE UNDER MY WATCH. I NOTICE YOU'VE GOT THIS MONSTROSITY--WHATEVER IT IS--READY TO LAUNCH...
YOU'LL FIND EVERYTHING YOU NEED TO KNOW IN HERE.

I DON'T THINK YOU'VE GOT ANY RIGHT TO BE PARANOID ABOUT THIS. THE JOINT CHIEFS ARE WILLING TO OFFER THIS ARRANGEMENT IN ALMOST COMPLETE ACCORDANCE WITH YOUR EXISTING BY-LAWS.
THAT MEANS YOUR SECRET IDENTITIES WILL REMAIN SECRET. AGAINST MY BETTER JUDGMENT...

THIS IS NEW TERRITORY FOR US, AGENT MURCH.
THE AVENGERS WERE A BIG HELP TO US IN ARIZONA. THE PRESIDENT HIMSELF SUGGESTED THIS MERGER...

...WORKING TOGETHER, THERE'S A LOT WE COULD ACCOMPLISH.

ARLINGTON NATIONAL CEMETERY; WASHINGTON, D.C.
In memory of
James
Buchanan
Barnes
Dec 13 1928
March 30 1945
Army Mascot
Camp Lehigh
BUCKY.

SO...
...ANY NAMES RING A BELL OUT THERE?
AS A MATTER OF FACT, YES.
CAN WE... TALK ALONE FOR A MINUTE?

IT'S STARTING TO COME BACK TO ME...MEMORIES, DETAILS...I KNOW I WAS THERE WHEN BUCKY WAS KILLED, BUT I STILL CAN'T REMEMBER HOW...OR WHO'S RESPONSIBLE...
MORE THAN THAT...SEEING ALL THESE HEADSTONES...SO MANY MORE THAN THE LAST TIME I WAS HERE. THIS COUNTRY SEEMS TO HAVE EXPERIENCED SO MUCH...
I WANT TO KNOW...

...WHAT ELSE HAS HAPPENED SINCE I'VE BEEN AWAY?

I DON'T BELIEVE YOU.
421-GOV

MURCH, IF YOU THINK I'M GOING TO JUMP BECAUSE YOU PARADE SOME ARMY BRASS UNDER MY NOSE...
I NEED TO CONSULT WITH MY TEAMMATES.
OH, PLEASE--!

I SHOULD HAVE MY HEAD EXAMINED!
I PRACTICALLY DELIVER YOUR PRECIOUS CLEARANCE ON A SILVER PLATTER, AND YOU HAVE THE TEMERITY TO QUESTION--

THEN I SHOULD TAKE IT THAT YOU'RE AGAINST US BEING POSSIBLE PAWNS OF THE MILITARY?
DOESN'T SOUND LIKE YOU, MURCH. I FIGURED YOU'D LOVE TO SEE US UNDER THE PENTAGON'S THUMB.

"PAWNS"...?!
THE ISSUE HERE IS NATIONAL SECURITY! I DON'T SEE HOW --

WHAT THE HELL'S GOING ON WITH THE WEATHER...?!

I WOULDN'T, AGENT MURCH...
I'LL BE GODDA--

AGENT MURCH...I'D LIKE YOU TO MEET THOR.
S-SOME LIGHT SHOW YOU...PUT ON THERE...
RIGHT. WELL...
...GUESS I NEED TO GET GOING.
YOU... UHHH...YOU THINK ABOUT THAT OFFER, IRON MAN...
YOU THINK ABOUT... R-RIGHT...
HAVE I EVER TOLD YOU HOW MUCH I APPRECIATE YOUR INNATE SENSE OF TIMING...?
AYE.
'TIS ALL ABOUT TIMING.
LET US ADJOURN TO THE GRAND HALL, AVENGER.
MINE INTUITION TELLS ME THERE IS MUCH TO DISCUSS.
YOU HAVE NO IDEA...

SO, THAT'S IT IN A NUTSHELL...
UNBELIEVABLE. THE U.S. ARMY WANTS TO PUT *US* ON THE PAYROLL!
SO WHAT'S THE UPSIDE?

WELL, FOR STARTERS, OUR *AVENGERS PRIORITY STATUS* WOULD BE GRANTED ALMOST IMMEDIATELY.
FROM THE BEGINNING, I TOLD YOU HOW *ESSENTIAL* THAT IS IF WE'RE TO DO OUR JOB WITH THE MINIMUM AMOUNT OF *INTERFERENCE...*

BUT YOU'RE TALKING ABOUT THE FREEDOM TO *ACT*. HOW MUCH FREEDOM ARE WE GOING TO HAVE UNDER *THIS* ARRANGEMENT?
I THINK WE NEED TO STOP AND CONSIDER WHAT THE PENTAGON *GAINS* FROM HAVING *US* AT THEIR BECK AND CALL...
...I DON'T THINK *ANY* OF US WANT TO END UP INVADING LIBYA OR SOME OTHER THIRD-WORLD NATION THE PRESIDENT *DISAGREES* WITH...

THERE IS *WISDOM* IN YOUR WORDS, GIANT-MAN.
THE SON OF ODIN IS NO MAN'S LACKEY. AND NO POLITICIAN HATH *EVER* PUT ANOTHER'S NEEDS ABOVE THEIR OWN.
WE MUST KEEP OUR *OWN* COUNSEL WHEN IT COMES TO SERVING THE GREATER GOOD.

SPEAKING OF KEEPING OUR OWN **COUNSEL**, THERE'S AN OPINION ***I'D*** REALLY LIKE TO HEAR...
...BUT IT LOOKS LIKE WE'RE AN AVENGER SHORT.
IF I MAY...
CAPTAIN AMERICA HAS TAKEN A FEW DAYS TO...***RE-FAMILIARIZE*** HIMSELF WITH CERTAIN AREAS OF AMERICAN HISTORY.
AND, I SUPPOSE, TO ***EDUCATE*** HIMSELF ON WHAT HAS TRANSPIRED IN HIS ***ABSENCE...***

VIETNAM VETERANS MEMORIAL
POW★MIA

UHHH, CAP...?
I WAS, UH, JUST ***WONDERING...*** HOW MUCH LONGER ARE WE GONNA ***BE*** HERE...?

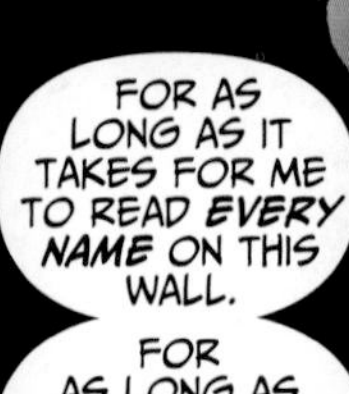
FOR AS LONG AS IT TAKES FOR ME TO READ ***EVERY NAME*** ON THIS WALL.

FOR AS LONG AS IT TAKES TO ACKNOWLEDGE ***EVERY SOLDIER*** THAT DIED...
...IN A WAR THAT I MISSED.

ONE WEEK LATER
DON'T HOLD BACK!
WE HAVE OUR ORDERS! LET'S MOVE IT!

WHA--?!
OUR ENEMIES HAVE ARRIVED!
YA GOT THAT RIGHT, GLOW-WORM!
GYEEARRGGH--!
PRESS YOUR ATTACK, "COMRADE"! SHE IS FAR TOO SMALL TO POSE ANY REAL THREAT!
OBSERVE HOW I STRIKE AT THEIR ACHILLES' HEEL!
VILE BRAGGART! THOU WOULDST FIRE UPON INNOCENT MORTALS?!
THOU ART TRULY MASTERS OF EVIL!
LUCKILY, WE DIDN'T COME UNPREPARED, PARTNER!

SCHNELL! WIR SIND AUF EINEM FESTEN ZEITPLAN!
OUR ENEMIES ARE CLOSE BY AND MY CONFIDENCE IN MY HIRED MINIONS IS WEAKENING BY THE SECOND.
DESTINY HAS BROUGHT ME TO THE NEW CITY...BUT THIS IS ERELY THE INITIAL SKIRMISH IN A MUCH LARGER WAR. FTER THIS OPENING SALVO, WHO WOULD DARE OPPOSE ME...?!
THEY'VE BAGGED THE RADIOACTIVE MAN!
THIS ENTIRE OPERATION IS SPIRALING OUT OF...
...CONTROL.

UNDERSTATEMENT OF THE YEAR, MELTER.

NO--!
STAY AWAY FROM ME! I'LL BRING THIS ENTIRE CITY DOWN ON YOUR HEAD--!

I'LL MAKE THIS OFFER UP FRONT...

...DROP YOUR WEAPONS AND SURRENDER NOW.
OTHERWISE, I'LL HAVE TO GET ROUGH.

THAT VOICE...
AFTER ALL THESE DECADES... I COULD NEVER FORGET THAT UNMISTAKABLE HINT OF AMERICAN NAIVETE.
BUT THE TRUE QUESTION REMAINS...
...DO YOU REMEMBER ME?
--EXPERIMENTAL DRONE PLANE--
WE'RE TOO LATE--
--I CAN REACH IT, CAP--!
--BOOBY-TRAPPED--
--IT'S GONNA BLOW--!
NOOOO--!!
ZEEEEEMO--!

HOW TOUCHING.
GEWEHR ER UNTEN WIE EIN HUND!
NOOOO--!
GHUURHNN--!

ODD'S BLOOD--!
HOW FARE THEE, AVENGERS?
I HAVE SUBDUED THE EVIL BLACK KNIGHT, BUT THE RINGLEADER OF THIS CACOPHONY HAS MADE HIS ESCAPE. SHALL I GIVE CHASE?
DON'T BOTHER, THOR.
I HAD CAP CHECKING THAT LAUNCH SITE AND GIANT-MAN HEADING IN FOR BACKUP. SPEAKING OF WHICH...
...GIANT-MAN, DO YOU COPY? OVER...
I'M RIGHT HERE, SHELLHEAD. THERE WASN'T MUCH TO DO...WHOEVER'S BEHIND ALL THIS WAS RUTHLESS ENOUGH TO SACRIFICE HIS OWN MEN DURING HIS GETAWAY.
AND CAP...?
HE'S...HERE, BUT NOT QUITE FIT FOR DUTY. I DON'T KNOW WHAT HAPPENED TO HIM, BUT WHATEVER IT WAS...
...IT WASN'T PRETTY.
...Z-ZEMO...

#4
KOLINS 04

"EACH TIME, IT'S ALWAYS SO *CLEAR*...
"IT'S LIKE... I CAN TASTE THE SALT OF MY *SWEAT*. I CAN FEEL THE *AIR* RUSHING PAST ME.
"AND THEN I *SEE* HIM...
"...AND SUDDENLY, I DON'T *CARE* IF IT'S A *DREAM* OR NOT.
"I JUST KEEP *MOVING*.
"I FORGET MYSELF. I FORGET WHAT I'M *FIGHTING* FOR. THIS OVERWHELMING *FEELING*... IT BECOMES ALL I *KNOW*.

"I JUST WANT..."
...I WANT HIM DEAD.
I'VE NEVER INTENTIONALLY TAKEN ANOTHER MAN'S LIFE... NOT EVEN IN WAR.
BUT ZEMO...

IT ALL CAME BACK TO ME UP ON THAT ROOFTOP. WHEN I SAW HIM...
...HEARD HIS VOICE...

YOU'RE LUCKY TO BE ALIVE, CAP. THAT BULLET--
I'M FINE. I'VE BEEN GRAZED BY GUNFIRE BEFORE.
I WOULD'VE TAKEN A THOUSAND BULLETS...
...JUST TO GET MY HANDS ON HIM.
AND NOW...
...IT'S ALMOST ALL I CAN THINK ABOUT, ASLEEP OR AWAKE.

TORTURED WARRIOR I WISH TO SEE FIGHTING AT MY SIDE. OUR CAMPAIGNS REQUIRE FOCUS--
FIRST THINGS FIRST, THOR.
YOU SAY IT ALL CAME BACK TO YOU... WHAT EXACTLY CAME BACK? WHAT DO YOU REMEMBER THAT YOU COULDN'T BEFORE?
I REMEMBER...
...EVERYTHING.
"WE'D TRACKED ZEMO ONTO AN E.T.O. BASE IN BRITAIN... HOME TO AN EXPERIMENTAL, AMERICAN-DESIGNED DRONE PLANE THAT WE KNEW THE NAZIS WERE DESPERATE TO GET THEIR HANDS ON...
"WELL... WE WERE JUST AS DESPERATE TO KEEP THEM FROM GETTING IT..."
WE'RE TOO LATE, BUCKY!
NO! DON'T STOP!
"ZEMO WAS HITLER'S GREATEST SCIENTIST... I COULDN'T COUNT HOW MANY OF HIS SCHEMES WE'D DEALT WITH ALREADY...
"BUT THIS TIME...
"...WAS DIFFERENT."
I THINK I CAN REACH IT, CAP--!
DON'T TRY TO GO IT ALONE!

MY PARTNER... BUCKY BARNES...
JUST A KID...!
"IT HAPPENED SO FAST..."
BUCKY-- LET GO!
YOU CAN'T--

ZEMO...
...HE KILLED HIM.
AND NOW HE'S OUT THERE RIGHT NOW.

INDEED.
THAT EXPLAINS THE MASTERS OF EVIL. THEY WANTED US OUT IN THE OPEN...OBVIOUSLY A TRAP SET BY ZEMO TO GET AT CAP...
HIS HOOD... I...

...DURING THE WAR, I DESTROYED A VAT OF ADHESIVE HE WAS DEVELOPING. IT... PERMANENTLY FUSED HIS HOOD TO HIS FACE. HE HATES ME FOR THAT.
AND NOW...

...I HATE HIM RIGHT BACK.
OH GOD...
...ANYONE THINK WE NEED TO GET IRON MAN IN ON THIS? WHERE IS HE, ANYWAY...?

THE ANSWER'S "NO."
I SEE.
TELL THE REST OF THE JOINT CHIEFS I'M SORRY, GENERAL WALLACE...
I DON'T BELIEVE THIS--!
I CAN'T SAY I'M NOT DISAPPOINTED, IRON MAN. I'D HOPED THIS WOULD BE AN ARRANGEMENT THAT BENEFITS US BOTH...
I UNDERSTAND. BUT MY TEAM-MATES AND I ARE IN COMPLETE AGREEMENT ABOUT THIS, REGARDLESS OF HOW IT AFFECTS OUR PRIORITY CLEARANCE...
...WE'LL WORK WITH YOU. NOT FOR YOU.
...FLUSHING IT RIGHT DOWN THE TOILET...!
WELL, IN THAT CASE...MAYBE YOU WOULDN'T MIND TAKING A LOOK AT THIS...
NASA SPY SATELLITES PICKED THIS UP OVER THE ATLANTIC LAST NIGHT. FOR AWHILE, IT WAS RADAR-INVISIBLE UNTIL IT SHOWED UP AGAIN OUTSIDE OF WAYNESBORO, OF ALL PLACES...
WE'VE GOT TROOPS MOVING IN, BUT I HAVE A FEELING THEY MAY NOT BE ENOUGH...

...ROGER THAT, CENTER. BEGINNING OUR DESCENT, OVER.
STRANGE CARGO, HUH...?
UNDERSTATEMENT OF THE YEAR. MAYBE THIS SPACESHIP'S COME TO PICK 'EM UP...
SO, HOW IS HE...?
KINDA IN HIS OWN WORLD, IF YOU ASK ME.
WE'RE TAKING A RISK HERE, SHELLHEAD IT'S LIKE HE'S FIXATED ON ZEMO. I DON'T KNOW HOW MUCH GOOD HE'LL BE TO US...
I MEAN, LOOK AT HIM. HE HASN'T SAID A WORD SINCE WE LEFT...
I HATE TO SAY IT, BUT YOU MIGHT BE RIGHT, HON.

I WAS WONDERING... IF I COULD G-GET A QUICK INTERVIEW...
...F-FOR STARS & STRIPES.
THEY STILL PUBLISH THAT...?
OKAY, SOLDIER...WHAT DO YOU WANT TO KNOW...?
I GUESS I WAS JUST WONDERING-- I MEAN, WE'RE ALL WONDERING--HERE YOU ARE, READY TO TAKE ON WHATEVER THIS THREAT MAY BE...
YOU'VE SEEN YOUR SHARE OF WAR. WE ALL KNOW IT. YOU'VE CERTAINLY EARNED THE RIGHT TO STOP. SO... WHY DO YOU KEEP DOING IT? WHAT'S LEFT TO FIGHT FOR...?

I...
...DON'T SEE THAT I HAVE A CHOICE, SOLDIER.
FORGET ABOUT MY PAST...WHAT I'VE BEEN THROUGH...THAT DOESN'T MATTER. THIS ISN'T ABOUT ME. IT NEVER WAS.
I WEAR THESE COLORS BECAUSE I BELIEVE IN SOMETHING GREATER THAN MYSELF. SOMETHING BIGGER...
AT SOME POINT IN LIFE, A MAN MAKES A DECISION...IS HE ALONE IN THIS WORLD OR ARE WE ALL IN THIS TOGETHER?
THOSE OF US IN THIS PLANE RIGHT NOW...HAVE MADE THAT DECISION.

I DON'T CARE WHAT DECADE IT IS. THE VALUES THAT THESE COLORS REPRESENT TRANSCEND SELFISHNESS...THEY TRANSCEND POLITICS...
IT'S ABOUT FREEDOM. THAT'S WHAT I FIGHT FOR. IT'S WHAT THE AVENGERS FIGHT FOR. AND I CAN'T EVER SEE MYSELF GIVING UP ON THAT.

AND SO, DESTINY CALLS MY NAME...
COUNTLESS CIVILIZATIONS HAVE BEEN TRAMPLED UNDER MY BOOT HEEL. NOW, ACROSS THE SEAS OF TIME ITSELF I HAVE SAILED...TO EMBRACE THE CONFLICT THAT LIVES WITHIN EVERY HUMAN HEART... TO PINPOINT THE PRECISE MOMENT OF MAXIMUM PSYCHOLOGICAL IMPACT.
AND HOW I WILL RELISH THIS MOMENT...
...AS I RETURN TO MY HOME PLANET DURING ITS GOLDEN AGE. THIS MOMENT IN HISTORY-- NEVER TO BE REPEATED-- IS MINE FOR THE TAKING.
THESE PRIMITIVES... THEY KNOW NOTHING OF DESTINY. THEY REVEL IN THE RANDOMNESS OF THEIR LIVES. I HAVE SEEN THIS TO BE THEIR GREATEST WEAKNESS...ONE TO BE EXPLOITED.
MY DESTINY IS PREORDAINED. AND IT SHALL BE FULFILLED. TO ASCEND TO GREATNESS... TO DOMINATE...
TO CONQUER.

FIVE HOURS LATER
...AFTER A BRIEF SKIRMISH, THE AVENGERS WERE TAKEN CAPTIVE BY THE MYSTERIOUS VISITOR KNOWN ONLY AS KANG.
THE WORLD WAITS ON ANY NEWS OF THEIR SURVIVAL AS KANG MAKES HIS TERRORIST DEMANDS.
CNN
NEVER HAS THE CONCEPT OF HEROISM BEEN MORE ELOQUENTLY DEFINED AS IT WAS BY CAPTAIN AMERICA MERE HOURS BEFORE BEING CAPTURED.
THIS AUDIO TAPE SUPPLIED BY A REPORTER FROM STARS & STRIPES CONTAINS PERHAPS THE LAST WORDS OF A LEGENDARY FIGURE...

...I BELIEVE IN SOMETHING GREATER THAN MYSELF. SOMETHING BIGGER...
FILE PHOTO
RECORDED VOICE OF
CAPTAIN AMERICA
...IT'S ABOUT FREEDOM. THAT'S WHAT I FIGHT FOR. IT'S WHAT THE AVENGERS FIGHT FOR. AND I CAN'T EVER SEE MYSELF GIVING UP ON THAT.

STIRRING WORDS FROM A LIVING ICON. AS THIS TEAM OF HEROES HAS POSSIBLY SACRIFICED THEMSELVES IN THE NAME OF HUMANITY, PUBLIC OPINION HAS SUDDENLY TURNED IN THEIR FAVOR...
EH...?

NINE HOURS LATER

THEY ARE TRYING MY PATIENCE.
I HAVE BESTED THEIR GREATEST CHAMPIONS, AND STILL THEY OFFER RESISTANCE.
HISTORY WILL RECORD THIS UPHEAVAL AS THE FIRST STEP TOWARD A NEW ERA. SOON, THE HUMAN RACE WILL FULLY COMPREHEND THEIR FATE...AND BOW DOWN BEFORE ME.
IRONICALLY, I HAVE DONE FOR THEM SOMETHING THEY HAVE NEVER DONE FOR THEMSELVES...
...I HAVE UNITED THEM. EVEN NOW, EACH AND EVERY NATION ON EARTH ENGAGES IN OPEN DIALOGUE ON HOW BEST TO DEAL WITH ME. ONLY IN TIMES OF WAR IS THERE FINALLY SERIOUS TALK OF PEACE.
I WILL GIVE THEM THEIR PEACE... BUT UNDER MY RULE.

BEWARE, TIME-TRAVELER...
...THINE ARROGANCE SHALL BE YOUR UNDOING.
YOU LABEL YOURSELF A CONQUEROR... AND YET YOUR ENEMY STANDS BEFORE YOU ONCE AGAIN, UNWILLING TO LIE DOWN. THE AVENGERS HAVE RETURNED TO DELIVER A SINGLE MESSAGE UNTO YOU ON BEHALF OF ALL OF MIDGARD...
...THOU ART UNWELCOME HERE.

THE FUTURE RARELY IS, "THUNDER GOD."
NOW... FEEL MY HATE!
WATCH IT--!
IGNORANT WHELPS...
...I HAVE A THOUSAND YEARS OF WARFARE TO DRAW UPON!
YOU'RE UP, THOR.
THE REST OF YOU... AVENGERS--
--ASSEMBLE!

YOUR IMPOTENCE AMUSES ME, AVENGERS...
THIS IS HOW YOU MAKE WAR...?!
NOT EXACTLY...
...BUT THIS IS.
THOR... DON'T LET UP NOW. I NEED A WEAK SPOT IN HIS FORCE FIELD...
AYE, GIANT-MAN--
--AND THOU SHALT HAVE IT--!
RIGHT THERE--!

N-NO--!
SOME SORT OF ACID...EATING THROUGH MY ARMOR...
DAMN YOU--
DAMN YOU ALL!!
WHAT NOW--?!
STAY WITH THIS MANIAC, PEOPLE--
--I'LL HANDLE THIS!

C'MON... C'MON--!
YOU THINK...YOU'VE WON...?!
I HAVE AN ENTIRE BATTERY OF NEUTRINO MISSILES TARGETING YOUR CENTERS OF CIVILIZATION!
MY VERY BEING SEETHES WITH THE RADIOACTIVITY YOUR ERA SO FEARS! I WILL SEE THIS PLANET BURN--
I SAY THEE NAY!
ENCHANTED MJOLNIR SHALL TAKE THAT WHICH YOU HOLD SO DEAR--!

WHA--?! N-NO!!
MY POWER... DRAINING...
...C-CAN'T...
THY MISERY IS JUST BEGINNING, KANG!
MINE IS ALSO THE POWER TO RETURN YOUR ENERGY TENFOLD!
YEEEARRHGG--!
...METHODS SO... PRIMITIVE...
HE'S MAKING A BREAK FOR IT!
DON'T LET HIM--

INTERNAL TRACKING SENSORS ARE GOING OFF THE CHARTS! WHAT IN GOD'S NAME--
'TIS A MORTAL-MADE WORMHOLE!
OUR ENEMY IS USING HIS MASTERY OF TIME TO MAKE HIS ESCAPE!
THAT'S IT, MEN!
ALL DIVISIONS-- MOVE IN!
--LIVE ON THE SCENE, AND I'D BE HARD-PRESSED TO ACCURATELY DESCRIBE TO YOU WHAT WE'RE WITNESSING HERE!
NEEDLESS TO SAY, I THINK THE SELF-STYLED CONQUEROR HAS DECIDED TO RETREAT!
GIANT-MAN--!
CAREFUL, PARTNERS... THE ENTIRE SHIP IS FOLLOWING KANG OUT OF EXISTENCE!
I CAN'T GET AN ACCURATE CHRONAL READING... IT'S WARPING TOO RAPIDLY--!
WHOA...!
RICK... WHAT YOU DID...
...OFFERING YOURSELF UP TO KANG TO GET ONTO THAT SHIP TO FREE US... IT WAS A RISK...
BUT I'M... PROUD OF YOU.
CAPTAIN AMERICA!
WE'RE LIVE ON ACTION NEWS 5! ANY COMMENT ON WHAT HAPPENED HERE TODAY?
DID THE AVENGERS JUST SAVE THE EARTH?

I'M NOT SURE WHAT--
THE ENTIRE WORLD HAS BEEN FOLLOWING THIS STORY! WE THOUGHT YOU MIGHT'VE BEEN KILLED!

FACING DEATH IS PART OF OUR JOB, MA'AM.
MY ONLY HOPE IS THAT PEOPLE UNDERSTAND THAT WE'RE HERE TO SERVE THEM.

WE DO THIS FOR THE SIMPLEST OF REASONS...BECAUSE IT'S THE RIGHT THING TO DO.
LET TODAY'S EVENTS SERVE AS A WARNING TO ANYONE WHO WOULD SEEK TO TERRORIZE HUMANITY...TO FORCE THEIR WILL UPON INNOCENT CITIZENS...
THE AVENGERS WON'T ALLOW IT.

LET'S GO, RICK.
NOT BAD...
...EVER THOUGHT ABOUT RUNNING FOR OFFICE?

GENERAL WALLACE...
...I'VE GOT THE PRESIDENT ON THE LINE.

MISTER PRESIDENT.
YES, SIR...
...THEY DID IT.

NEW YORK CITY; FOUR DAYS LATER
AVENGERS
I FIND THIS MORTAL DISPLAY OF GRATITUDE TO BE... EXCESSIVE.
MAYBE IT IS, THOR...
...BUT YOU HAVE NO IDEA HOW MUCH THIS IS GOING TO HELP US.
THERE'S NOTHING SO POWERFUL AS GOOD P.R....

THAT WHOLE "KANG" NONSENSE CAST YOUR CREW AS WORLDWIDE SAVIORS.
YOU'D CERTAINLY HAVE THE PEOPLE'S SYMPATHY IF YOU DECIDED TO TALK PUBLICLY ABOUT HOW THE U.S. GOVERNMENT IS JERKING YOU AROUND ON YOUR SPECIALIZED SECURITY CLEARANCE...
BUT THERE'S NO NEED FOR THAT...IS THERE, MURCH...?
I HAVE TO HAND IT TO YOU, IRON MAN...
...YOU PULLED YOUR FAT OUT OF THE FIRE.
...
NO. THERE'S NOT.
MY SUPERIORS WANT ME TO MAKE IT CLEAR TO YOU...WHATEVER PRIVILEGES THAT ARE GRANTED EXIST AT THE DISCRETION OF THE NATIONAL SECURITY COUNCIL. HAVING SAID THAT...
...YOU CAN EXPECT YOUR A-1 PRIORITY STATUS TO GO INTO EFFECT WITHIN TWENTY-FOUR HOURS.
YOU'LL BE ISSUED I.D. CARDS... AND WE'LL BE LOOKING INTO WAYS TO VERIFY YOUR IDENTITIES WITHOUT COMPROMISING ANY... SECRETS YOU EACH MAY HAVE.
I'M HAPPY TO HEAR THE NSC HAS COME AROUND.
I CAN HEAR THAT SMUG SMIRK IN YOUR VOICE, BUT I SHOULD INFORM YOU OF THE COUNCIL'S MOST PERTINENT RESTRICTION ON GRANTING YOUR CLEARANCE...
...CAPTAIN AMERICA.
IF, FOR ANY REASON, HE DECIDES TO LEAVE YOUR ACTIVE ROSTER, I DOUBT MY BOSSES WOULD HAVE ANY PROBLEM WITH IMMEDIATELY RESCINDING SAID CLEARANCE. AND THIS POINT IS NON-NEGOTIABLE.
SO, YOU'VE GOT YOUR A-1 PRIORITY STATUS...AS LONG AS CAP STAYS.

HOW FARE THEE, AVENGER...?
HAS THE HEAT OF BATTLE SOOTHED THY BROODING NATURE...?
I WISH IT HAD, THOR.
I CAN PUT UP A GOOD FRONT, THAT'S FOR SURE...
I DON'T...EVEN WANT TO SLEEP ANYMORE. THE NIGHTMARES--
THE OCCASIONAL THIRST FOR REVENGE IS PART OF A WARRIOR'S HEART...ESPECIALLY WHEN THY BRETHREN HATH BEEN TAKEN FROM YOU...
THE SON OF ODIN KNOWS.
WE SHOULD BE BETTER THAN THAT.
I DON'T THINK BUCKY WOULD THINK TOO HIGHLY OF ME RIGHT NOW...SO PREOCCUPIED WITH THOUGHTS OF HIS KILLER'S DEATH...
...BUT I JUST CAN'T HELP MYSELF.
I DON'T THINK I'VE EVER WANTED ANYTHING SO BADLY.

I'M AFRAID THAT...UNTIL I SEE ZEMO *DEAD...*
...I DON'T KNOW HOW MUCH LONGER I'LL BE ABLE TO *FUNCTION.*
THY DEMONS RUN *DEEP,* CAPTAIN AMERICA.
HAVE A CARE THEY DO NOT *OVERTAKE* YOU. PERHAPS THE *CURE* LIES IN *FULFILLING* THE DESTINY THY DREAMS ARE *PROPHESIZING.*
WHAT ARE YOU *SAYING...?*
THAT I SHOULD *DELIBERATELY* SEEK HIM OUT AND...
...AND...

#5
KOLINS 04

THE BRONX
...IF HE REFUSES TO COMPLY, I'LL CALL YOUR BUILDING SUPER, AND WE'LL MAKE SURE IT GETS FIXED.
IF YOU INSIST, SON.
YOU LOOK TIRED. I HOPE THAT MR. STARK ISN'T WORKING YOU TOO HARD.
WELL, MOTHER, I'M NOT QUITE WORKING FOR MR. STARK ANYMORE. THAT IS...I AM, BUT IN A DIFFERENT CAPACITY...ACTUALLY...
WHAT ARE YOU TRYING TO TELL ME, EDWIN?
ERRR...
I...THINK WE'RE READY FOR THE CHECK...
...AND YOU COOK FOR THESE STRANGE PEOPLE?
AMONG OTHER THINGS, YES. HAVEN'T YOU BEEN WATCHING TELEVISION, MOTHER? THE NEWS PROGRAMS...?
YOU KNOW I ONLY WATCH PUBLIC TELEVIS --
HOLD UP, GRANNY.
OH--!
'DIS Y'LUCKY NIGHT.
DO NOT FEED
NO--!

UNHAND HER! IF IT'S MONEY YOU WANT --
SHUT IT, OLD MAN!
I'LL KILL THIS SKEEVY DUSTBAG...
GUH...!
HHNNGGGGG--!
UTT--!
E-EDWIN--!
WHAT...
...WHAT JUST HAPPENED HERE...?!
DO ME A FAVOR, POPS...

...WHEN YOU TALK TO THE COPS ABOUT THIS, TELL 'EM THAT HAWKEYE WAS THE GOOD GUY, WILLYA?
I DON'T NEED ANY MORE BAD PRESS.
"HAWKEYE"...?
YOU TWO OKAY...?
Y'KNOW, I USUALLY DON'T MAKE IT UP HERE TO THE BRONX...GUESS IT WAS FATE, HUH...?
I'M...NOT SURE WHAT TO SAY...
THANK YOU.
HEY, DON'T MENTION IT. IT'S ALL PART OF THE JOB...NO MATTER WHAT THE FUZZ THINKS ABOUT ME...
YOU FOLKS TAKE CARE.
WAIT--!
PLEASE...

ALL MEN WEAR MASKS.
NEW JERSEY
THIS IS THE WAY OF THE WORLD. WE CLOAK OURSELVES IN THOSE THINGS THAT WOULD BEST PROVIDE FOR US. BUT, AS I SAY, THEY ARE ALL MERELY MASKS. RESPECTABILITY... NOBILITY...
...HEROISM.
BUT BEHIND THESE MASKS... WE ARE ALL OF ONE FACE.
IF YOU TRULY BELIEVE THAT, NEFARIA...
...YOU'RE MORE TWISTED THAN I THOUGHT.

FORGIVE ME IF I TAKE ISSUE WITH YOUR NOTION OF "HOSPITALITY", COUNT...
RELEASE CAPTAIN AMERICA. OR ELSE.
YOUR THREATS ARE PITIABLE.
KILL HIM..!
RIGHT.
YOU'RE DOING ABOUT AS WELL AS YOUR LACKEYS OUTSIDE...

C'MON-- THIS WAY!
WE'RE RUNNIN' IN CIRCLES, JONES! QUIT ACTING LIKE YOU CAN GET US OUTTA THIS DUNGEON--!
YE OF LITTLE FAITH--
WHOA--!
RICK!
DIDN'T WE TELL YOU TO STAY AWAY FROM THIS PLACE?!
I KNOW, I KNOW!
LOOK... WE JUST WANTED TO HELP. YOU KNOW NEFARIA'S A SICKO! AND WITH ALL THE MILITARY BUILDUP OUTSIDE, WE FIGURED YOU GUYS--
ALL RIGHT, FINE. YOU CAN EXPLAIN LATER. RIGHT NOW, WE'VE GOT TO--
OH, GOD--!
THERE THEY ARE--!

BOTTOM OF THE BARGE
IT'S FUNNY HOW LIFE TURNS OUT...
...WHO WOULDA THOUGHT I'D BE SHOWING THE AVENGERS' BUTLER A LITTLE BIT OF LIFE ON THE WRONG SIDE OF THE TRACKS, HUH...?
INDEED.
YOU... EAT HERE OFTEN?
DECENT FOOD FOR THE RIGHT PRICE. I'M NOT EXACTLY MAKING A MINT IN THE "ROBIN HOOD" GAME SO FAR...
BESIDES, IT'S IN MY BEST INTERESTS TO KEEP A LOW PROFILE...
WELL, THEN... AREN'T YOU EVEN SLIGHTLY NERVOUS...? YOUR UNIFORM...
AHHH, NONE A' THE DRUNKS IN HERE ARE PAYIN' ANY ATTENTION.
AND EVEN IF THEY WERE, THEY WOULDN'T CARE. I THINK WE'RE OKAY.
I SEE.
SO, THIS CLANDESTINE LIFESTYLE SERVES SOME PURPOSE FOR YOU.
YOU'RE RUNNING FROM THE LAW...?

YOU COULD SAY THAT.
THE COPS AND I... WELL, THEY'RE LABORING UNDER A BIT OF A MISUNDERSTANDING.
ONE OF MY FIRST OUTINGS...I BUSTED UP A JEWELRY HEIST. COPS SHOWED UP...THOUGHT I WAS PART OF IT...
I EVEN HAD A FEW RUN-INS WITH YOUR BOY, IRON MAN... NOW THERE WAS A BIG MISUNDERSTANDING.
I GUESS... THINGS HAVE GOTTEN A LITTLE OUT OF HAND. I STARTED OUT... WELL, I WANTED TO DO THE WHOLE HERO THING, Y'KNOW...? DO WHAT YOU GUYS DO. MAYBE NOT ON THAT SCALE, BUT I WANTED TO DO MY BIT...
CRAZY WORLD OUT THERE...
YES, IT IS. VERY MUCH SO.
HEY, LOOK... I AIN'T CRYIN' ABOUT IT. I'LL DO WHAT I DO, AND IF I GOTTA TAKE A FEW LUMPS, THEN SO BE IT.
I KNOW WHAT I'M ABOUT. I KNOW I'M NO CROOK. I JUST THOUGHT... I'D END UP BEING PART OF SOMETHING. INSTEAD, I'M OUT HERE PRETTY MUCH ON MY OWN...
AH, WHATEVER.
LEMME JUST PAY THE CHECK AND WE CAN GET THE HELL OUTTA HERE...
PLEASE.
ALLOW ME...

MANHATTAN
...BUT CAN YOU BLAME ME? I MEAN, JARVIS... YOU SHOULD SEE THIS WOMAN...!
YOUR DESCRIPTION PAINTS QUITE THE PICTURE...
...BUT SURELY YOU SEE THAT THIS AFFAIR HAS CONTRIBUTED TO YOUR CURRENT DILEMMA.
WELL, SURE. WHADDYA WANT ME TO SAY...? GUILTY AS CHARGED. BUT THE SEX--
IF I MAY... HOW SERIOUS ARE YOU ABOUT YOUR CRIME-FIGHTING CAREER?
AND DON'T HUSTLE ME. I CAN SEE RIGHT THROUGH YOUR BRAVADO. HONESTLY, IT DOESN'T HELP YOUR CAUSE AT ALL...
YEAH...
...WELL, BEING A LOUDMOUTH WORKS FOR ME, OKAY? I'M PRETTY MUCH RESIGNED TO THE FACT THAT I'LL NEVER GET A ROOM IN THE MANSION, ANYWAY...
...SPEAKING OF WHICH, WHY BRING ME ALL THE WAY UP HERE? TO RUB MY NOSE IN IT...?
NOT EXACTLY, MR. HAWKEYE.
I'VE ACTUALLY GOT SOMETHING ELSE IN MIND...

THOR! DON'T--!
CONNIVING VILLAIN! THOU SHALT TASTE THE STONE OF MJOLNIR!
I SHALL GRIND YOUR BONES INTO MIDGARD DUST!
COMPANY! SECURE THE AREA!
MOVE IT! MOVE IT! MOVE IT--!
NO--!
HERE WE GO... I'VE HACKED INTO NEFARIA'S ENCRYPTED FILES. HARD DRIVE'S SELF-CORRUPTING, BUT I THINK I'VE PUT A FREEZE ON IT.
JUST GIVE ME A FEW MORE SECONDS HERE...
SIR!
THIS HIM?
SOMEBODY GET ME CAPTAIN AMERICA SO WE CAN FIGURE OUT WHAT THE HELL'S GOING ON HERE...!
GIANT-MAN...?
IT'S FINE. I DID AN INFO DUMP BEFORE THE SYSTEM CRASHED.
THIS DATA CONFIRMS NEFARIA'S STATUS AS HEAD OF THE MAGGIA...

...PLENTY OF EVIDENCE THERE FOR A CONVICTION. UNLESS THERE'S SOME CONCERN ABOUT DIPLOMATIC IMMUNITY...
OH, I DON'T THINK THAT'LL BE AN ISSUE, CAP. I WANT TO SEE THIS MEGALOMANIAC TAKEN DOWN...
SO DO WE, GENERAL.
IS EVERYTHING COPASETIC WITH THE ARMY NOW...?
AS WELL AS IT CAN BE, I SUPPOSE. FOR A WHILE, THEY WERE CONVINCED WE WERE IN LEAGUE WITH NEFARIA--
WAIT A MINUTE... WHERE'S THE WASP?!
...SURE SHE FOUND RICK, NO PROBLEM.
THEN WHY CAN'T WE RAISE HER ON THE COMM LINK...?!
KKKKK -- ANYBODY READ ME?! I'M ON THE WASP'S HEADSET! WE NEED SOME HELP DOWN HERE!
SOMEBODY, PLEASE! HURRY --
RICK? WE'RE LOCKED ON YOUR SIGNAL...

OH, MY GOD...!
...IT... HAPPENED SO FAST... NEFARIA'S GOONS... THEY...
S-SHE...
...GOT SHOT.

EAST TRANSIA, EUROPE
THIS IS INTOLERABLE...!
LET'S EAT QUICKLY AND GET MOVING AGAIN. WE CAN'T AFFORD TO STAY STILL FOR VERY LONG...

LUCKILY, WE'VE COVERED OUR TRACKS WELL. I'M SURE HE DOESN'T KNOW WHERE WE ARE...
FROM HERE, WE CAN CROSS THE BORDER INTO ROMANIA BY DAWN--
PIETRO, PLEASE...
...HOW MUCH LONGER ARE WE TO LIVE AS FUGITIVES...?
SISTER, ARE YOU INSANE?!
WE ARE MORE THAN FUGITIVES! THE ENTIRE WORLD SEES US AS NOTHING MORE THAN MUTANT OUTLAWS... WHAT CHOICE DO WE HAVE?!
I UNDERSTAND. I REALLY DO. BUT WE'RE NOT CRIMINALS...
...WE DESERVE BETTER THAN THIS.
YOU'RE RIGHT, WANDA.
BUT I'M AFRAID WE'VE RUN OUT OF OPTIONS. NO MATTER WHAT OUR INTENTIONS MAY BE...
...THEY WILL NEVER ALTER THEIR PERCEPTION OF US. TO THEM...
...WE ARE PURE EVIL.

I NEED A DOCTOR!
NOW!

PLEASE... SOMEONE...
NURSE! 'TIS A GSW TO THE CHEST...HER PULSE IS 40 PALP. START AN I.V.... TYPE AND CROSSMATCH...
FOLKS, GIVE US SOME ROOM HERE...!

DEAR GOD, I JUST HOPE WE'RE NOT TOO LATE...
IT'S NOT WORTH...
...I MEAN... YES, SO DO I.

SOMEBODY GET A DAMN DOCTOR OVER HERE--!

OKAY, I'VE GOT THE LATEST...
...NOW THAT DOCTOR SVENSON'S HERE, THE WASP IS IN SURGERY. ALL WE CAN DO...IS WAIT.
I SUPPOSE SO.
SHE'S CRITICAL, BUT SVENSON'S THE BEST IN HIS FIELD.
I HONESTLY NEVER THOUGHT IT WOULD COME TO THIS...
WE'VE GOT STRENGTH IN NUMBERS. THAT WAS THE WHOLE IDEA HERE. I SUPPOSE I FIGURED...TOGETHER, WE MIGHT JUST BE UNTOUCHABLE.
SO FAR, WE'VE BEEN PRETTY GOOD AT OUR JOB. BUT IS LOSING ONE OF OUR OWN TOO HIGH A PRICE TO PAY...?
I THINK I NEED SOME AIR--
CAP... WAIT.

I...NEED TO TALK TO YOU ABOUT SOMETHING.
YOU KNOW WE FINALLY GOT OUR SECURITY CLEARANCE. THIS GOVERNMENT WEASEL, MURCH...I'M CONVINCED HE'S GOT IT IN FOR US...
THE THING IS... THE NSC HAS PLACED A SINGLE RESTRICTION ON OUR--
IRON MAN... I CAN'T DO THIS RIGHT NOW.
YOU'RE ASKING ME TO THINK ABOUT ADMINISTRATIVE REGULATIONS AND PENTAGON PAPERWORK, BUT THE TRUTH IS...
...THERE'S ONLY ONE THING I'M INTERESTED IN RIGHT NOW.
ZEMO.
HE'S STILL AT LARGE.
AND ALL I CAN THINK ABOUT IS FINDING HIM...AND ENDING THIS CIRCLE OF VIOLENCE ONCE AND FOR ALL.
CAP, MAYBE WE CAN--
DON'T.
I'VE NEVER BEEN THE TYPE TO BROOD. BUT THIS IS BEGINNING TO AFFECT MY WORK IN THE FIELD. THIS IS MY NIGHTMARE... NOT YOURS.
I NEVER WOULD'VE LET MYSELF BE TAKEN PRISONER BEFORE...NOT BY SOME TWO-BIT DESPOT LIKE NEFARIA...!
WHO CAN SAY IF MY MISTAKE WON'T END UP COSTING THE WASP HER LIFE...

I'VE NEVER FELT THIS KIND OF... PAIN BEFORE. I'VE NEVER...HATED LIKE THIS...
AND I'VE NEVER WANTED TO ENACT THE KIND OF RETRIBUTION THAT EVEN HAUNTS MY DREAMS...!
IT'S AS THOUGH THE CHOICE HAS COME DOWN TO ZEMO'S LIFE...OR MY OWN SOUL.
I NEED TO MAKE THAT CHOICE...
...AND I NEED TO MAKE IT SOON.
DEAR GOD...!
THERE IS NO DISHONOR IN ANGUISHING OVER A LOVED ONE...

...BUT NEITHER MORTAL NOR GOD HAS YET DECIDED HER FATE. IN MATTERS SUCH AS THESE...
...ONE MUST HAVE FAITH.
IS THAT... SUPPOSED TO MAKE ME FEEL BETTER...?
NAY, AVENGER. 'TIS MERELY THE TRUTH.
THE GATES OF VALHALLA HAVE WELCOMED MANY A NOBLE WARRIOR. WHEN THE WASP'S TIME COMES, SHE WILL HAVE HER SEAT IN THE GREAT HALL...
...BUT MINE INTUITION TELLS ME THIS IS NOT HER TIME.
YOU'VE GOT A HELLUVA NERVE, THOR!
TO STAND IN HERE AND PLAY THAT PIOUS "GODHOOD" ACT WHEN MY JAN COULD BE IN THERE DYING!
'TIS NO ACT.
AND I WOULD NOT HESITATE TO CALL UPON THE ALL-FATHER TO INTERVENE IN MATTERS WHERE MY TEAMMATES ARE CONCERNED.

THE "ALL-FATHER"... SURE...
WELL, THAT'S A REAL RELIEF, THOR...BUT I'D RATHER DEAL WITH REALITY, IF YOU DON'T MIND.
I SWEAR, IF SHE SURVIVES... I'LL GET HER AWAY FROM ALL THIS MADNESS...
SHE NEVER WANTED THIS LIFE. DEAR LORD... PLEASE...!
THOU WOULDST REJECT THY DESTINY? YOUR PLACE--BOTH OF YOU--IS AMONG WARRIORS OF EQUAL METTLE.
FORGET IT! I DON'T NEED YOUR EMPTY PLATITUDES!
Y'KNOW... YOU CLAIM TO BE A "GOD", BUT I DON'T SEE YOU STEPPING UP TO PERFORM ANY MIRACLES HERE--!
AHEM--!
AM I... INTERRUPTING SOMETHING...?
DOCTOR SVENSON! WHAT'S GOING ON WITH JAN?!
TELL ME--
S-SHE'S IN RECOVERY RIGHT NOW...
THE OPERATION WAS SUCCESSFUL.
SHE'S GOING TO BE FINE.

THAT'S FANTASTIC!
INDEED IT IS.
INJURIES ARE TO BE EXPECTED IN THEIR LINE OF WORK, BUT ONE OF THIS SEVERITY...
THE WASP'S A TOUGH COOKIE. YOU KNOW SHE'LL BE BACK IN THE SADDLE IN NO TIME...
I WOULD IMAGINE SO.
ONE TENDS TO FORGET HOW THEY PUT THEIR LIVES ON THE LINE EVERY SINGLE DAY...
HEY, THE HERO GAME'S A RISKY BUSINESS. YOU GOTTA--
UHHH...
JARVIS...?
GOT KINDA DARK IN HERE...
THAT'S ODD.
THE SECURITY GRID DOESN'T SEEM TO BE RESPONDING TO MY OVERRIDE CODE...
PERHAPS THERE'S A --
GUHD--!
JARVIS--!
WEEP NOT FOR THE HIRED HELP, BOY. HIS MURDER IS BENEATH ME.
AS IS YOURS. YOU ARE LESS THAN NOTHING.

YOU ARE BUT A MEANS TO AN END.

#6
KEEP OUT

--WASN'T SURE IT WAS THEM UNTIL I GOT A CLOSER LOOK. BUT I CAN CONFIRM...IT WAS THE ENCHANTRESS AND THE EXECUTIONER!
I LOST THEM AT THE CORNER OF 58TH AND PARK AVENUE, HEADING WEST. I'M ON MY WAY BACK NOW...
REPEAT: THIS IS CAPTAIN AMERICA ON AVENGERS PRIORITY CHANNEL ALPHA--
SO...
...WHAT ARE WE GOING TO TELL HIM?
THEY ATTACKED ME FROM BEHIND, SIR... IF ONLY I'D SEEN IT COMING, I COULD'VE--
FOR THE LAST TIME... IT WASN'T YOUR FAULT, JARVIS. THERE WAS NOTHING YOU COULD'VE DONE TO PREVENT IT. FRANKLY, YOU'RE LUCKY TO BE ALIVE.
SOMEHOW ZEMO CIRCUMVENTED THE MANSION'S SECURITY SYSTEMS...
HOW I WISH THEY'D TAKEN ME INSTEAD OF YOUNG MISTER JONES...! YOU HAVE NO IDEA...
PERHAPS I SHOULD TELL HIM, SIR.
NO...
...I'LL DO IT.

SO THAT'S IT, THEN.
LOOK...I KNOW WHAT YOU MUST BE FEELING RIGHT NOW. RICK'S AN INNOCENT IN ALL THIS...
ZEMO'S OBVIOUSLY USING HIM TO GET TO YOU.
GUESS IT WORKED.
IT GETS... DIFFICULT TO MAINTAIN CIVILIAN RELATIONSHIPS. THEY INEVITABLY BECOME TARGETS.
BUT WE HAVE A RESPONSIBILITY TO--
I'VE ALREADY SPOKEN TO NICK FURY OVER AT THE C.I.A.
HE'S BEEN GATHERING INTELLIGENCE REPORTS ON ZEMO'S LAST KNOWN WHEREABOUTS. SOMEWHERE IN SOUTH AMERICA, THEY THINK...
CAP...
...ARE YOU LISTENING TO ME...?

IF THE ENCHANTRESS AND THE EXECUTIONER ARE STILL IN THE *CITY*--
ZEMO WANTS TO FORCE MY HAND.
HE'S OBVIOUSLY AS COMMITTED TO *ENDING* THIS AS I AM. HE WANTS HIS *REVENGE...*
...AND SO DO I.

LISTEN TO ME, PLEASE...
...IF THE MASTERS OF EVIL ARE *OUT THERE,* THEN IT'S CLEAR THAT ZEMO WANTS TO ENGAGE US ON MULTIPLE FRONTS. HE'S LOOKING TO DIVIDE AND CONQUER.
WE'VE *SEEN* WHAT THEY CAN DO WHEN THEY WANT TO GET OUR ATTENTION. WE'RE TALKING POSSIBLE CIVILIAN CASUALTIES ON A *MASSIVE SCALE.*

I KNOW THERE'S A *DIFFICULT CHOICE* TO BE MADE HERE. I FEEL AS RESPONSIBLE FOR RICK'S KIDNAPPING AS *YOU* DO.

BUT DON'T WE HAVE A *DUTY* TO--
THERE *IS* NO CHOICE FOR ME. I WON'T LET WHAT HAPPENED *BEFORE...*
...HAPPEN AGAIN.

FINE. BUT I HAVEN'T FORGOTTEN THE THINGS YOU TOLD ME BACK IN THE HOSPITAL.
YOU BASICALLY ADMITTED YOUR OBSESSION. HOW IT'S KEEPING YOU UP AT NIGHT... AND HOW IT'S AFFECTED YOUR WORK.

SO LEVEL WITH ME. ONCE AND FOR ALL...
...IS THIS REALLY ABOUT RICK OR IS ITJUST ABOUT ZEMO...?

ALL RIGHT, THEN...
WELL...LET'S GET EVERYBODY TO THE HANGAR. WE'LL WARM UP THE NEW QUINJET AND TRY A TRACE SIGNAL ON RICK'S PHYSIOLOGICAL--

WAIT...

...DON'T BOTHER.
WHAT NEEDS TO BE DONE... I NEED TO DO IT ALONE.

ZEMO WON'T HESITATE TO KILL RICK. THAT'LL ONLY BE THE BEGINNING...
THE LONGER I WAIT, THE WORSE IT'LL GET.
NOW HOLD ON A MINUTE--
THE REST OF YOU SHOULD STAY. DEAL WITH WHATEVER THE MASTERS OF EVIL ARE GOING TO THROW AT YOU...
...BUT I HAVE TO DO THIS.
LIKE I SAID, I JUST...DON'T HAVE A CHOICE. NOT ANYMORE.
CAP, YOU NEED TO UNDERSTAND SOMETHING. YOUR AVENGERS MEMBERSHIP HAS MEANT A LOT. NOT ONLY TO US...
...BUT TO THE NATIONAL SECURITY COUNCIL. FINALLY OBTAINING OUR PRIORITY STATUS WAS CONTINGENT UPON YOUR INVOLVEMENT.
THEY MADE IT PERFECTLY CLEAR TO ME...WITHOUT YOU, THEY WON'T HESITATE TO YANK THAT SECURITY CLEARANCE WITHOUT BATTING AN EYE.
SO IF YOU WALK OUT THAT DOOR... YOU'RE RISKING EVERYTHING WE'VE BUILT HERE.
I'M SORRY, IRON MAN.
I REALLY AM.

DAMN.
OH.
JARVIS.
YOU HEARD...?
ONLY BY ACCIDENT, I ASSURE YOU, SIR. YOU KNOW I WOULD NEVER INTENTIONALLY EAVESDROP ON A PRIVATE--
NO NEED TO APOLOGIZE. BUT I WILL SAY THIS...
...DON'T MENTION THIS TO ANYONE. IF WORD GETS OUT THAT CAP IS AWOL, WE'RE SUNK.
ALTHOUGH, AT THIS POINT, THAT MAY BE AN INEVITABILITY.

ROOKLYN
HOW'D YOU FIND ME...?
WAIT. DON'T TELL ME. PROBABLY TRACKED ME DOWN WITH SOME SUPERCOMPUTER YOU KEEP NEXT TO THE FINE CHINA...
SOMETHING LIKE THAT.
MAY I ASK... HOW DO YOU OBTAIN THE TECHNOLOGY FOR YOUR ARROWHEADS...?
WELL, I'VE TAKEN DOWN A DRUG DEALER OR TWO. THERE'S USUALLY A BIT OF CASH LYING AROUND AFTER A BUST LIKE THAT...
..THEN I GO TO THIS GUY, PHINEAS MASON. HE SPECIALIZES IN THIS KIND OF THING. TECH STUFF, HARD-TO-FIND WEAPONRY, ONE-OF-A-KIND WORKMANSHIP...
...THEY CALL HIM THE TINKERER.
A KNOWN CRIMINAL.
THERE ARE MORE SENSIBLE WAYS OF ARMING YOURSELF.
YEAH, WHATEVER.
Y'KNOW... NOT EVERYONE HAS ACCESS TO TONY STARK'S BANK ACCOUNT. SOME OF US JUST HAVE TO MAKE DO...

HEY!
WHO THE HELL ARE YOU TO TELL ME WHAT'S WHAT?! YOU THINK I DON'T KNOW I'M HANGIN' ON BY MY FINGERNAILS HERE?!
WHO AM I?! I'M THE ONE WHO WANTS TO HELP YOU PULL YOURSELF OUT OF THIS DEAD-END SITUATION!
IF YOU WEREN'T SO HORRIBLY ARROGANT, MAYBE YOU'D SEE THAT!
YOU GONNA DO FAIRY ...?
GOT NO WHAT I AM, VIS. THIS IS MY LIFE...
...IT'S NOT LIKE I CAN DO MUCH TO CHANGE IT!

HELLO...?
SOMEONE IN HERE...?
AYE.
THOR...
...WHAT IN GOD'S NAME ARE YOU DOING SITTING ALL ALONE? THE LAST THING WE NEED AROUND HERE IS MORE STRANGE BEHAVIOR...!
I GUESS I DON'T HAVE TO TELL YOU...CAP'S ABRUPT DEPARTURE HAS PUT US IN A PRECARIOUS POSITION.
I DON'T KNOW IF HE'S EVER COMING BACK. AND THAT MEANS...PRETTY SOON MURCH IS GOING TO START SNIFFING AROUND AGAIN.
WE'VE WORKED SO HARD...COME SO FAR. IF HE FOLLOWS THROUGH ON HIS THREAT TO STRIP US OF OUR SECURITY CLEARANCE JUST BECAUSE CAP'S GONE...
...I'M JUST NOT SURE IF WE'LL BE ABLE TO HOLD IT TOGETHER--
BEFORE YOU GO ANY FURTHER, THERE IS SOMETHING YOU SHOULD KNOW...
...I, TOO, MUST TAKE MY LEAVE.
EFFECTIVE IMMEDIATELY.

WH-WHAT...?!
THOR... WHY IN THE WORLD WOULD YOU PICK NOW, OF ALL TIMES, TO TAKE OFF?! YOUR TIMING COULDN'T BE WORSE!
WHEN WILL YOU--
THERE ARE MATTERS ELSEWHERE WHICH REQUIRE MY ATTENTION.
AND THUS... THERE IS A POSSIBILITY THAT I SHALL NOT RETURN AT ALL.
I TRULY REGRET THIS TURN OF EVENTS. BUT THERE ARE TIMES WHEN EVEN A THUNDER GOD MUST ANSWER A HIGHER CALLING.
DON'T TELL ME THIS HAS SOMETHING TO DO WITH "ASGARD" AND "ODIN" AND THIS MYTHICAL PANTHEON OF "GODS" YOU CLAIM TO COME FROM...!
YOU'RE HANGING US OUT TO DRY!
'TIS NO "CLAIM" I MAKE. 'TIS MERELY THE TRUTH.
MY EXALTED FATHER HATH COMMANDED A TRIAL OF THE GODS, AND I AM DUTY-BOUND TO HEED HIS WORD.
AND WHAT ABOUT YOUR DUTY TO US?! TO WHAT WE'VE STRUGGLED TO ACCOMPLISH HERE?!
I CAN SWALLOW YOUR HIGH AND MIGHTY ATTITUDE... MOSTLY BECAUSE I THOUGHT YOUR COMMITMENT WAS WITHOUT QUESTION!
OR WERE ALL THOSE HAUGHTY PROCLAMATIONS JUST ANOTHER PART OF THIS FANTASY WORLD YOU SEEM TO BE LIVING IN--
HAVE CARE, IR MAN.

YOU HAVE PROVEN YOURSELF TO BE ONE OF THE NOBLEST WARRIORS I HAVE EVER ENCOUNTERED...
...BUT THINE HOSTILITY HAS YOU ONCE AGAIN QUESTIONING THE VALIDITY OF MY ORIGINS. AS A FELLOW AVENGER, MINE HOPE HAS ALWAYS BEEN THAT I BE TAKEN AT MY WORD.
IF THOU STILL DOST REQUIRE PROOF OF EXACTLY WHERE I HAIL FROM, THEN YOU SHALL HAVE IT...
...PLACE THINE HAND UPON MJOLNIR. LET THE POWER OF ODIN'S ENCHANTMENT ENTER THY MIND'S EYE, SO THOU SHALT WITNESS WHAT MINE EYES HAVE SEEN.
WHAT ARE YOU...
...

WUH--!
GOOD GOD...!
YOU HAVE GAZED UPON SIGHTS NO OTHER MORTAL HAS.
YOU HAVE SEEN THE GLORY THAT IS ASGARD.
WAIT A MINUTE...
YOU REALLY ARE--
AYE...
...'TIS NO FABRICATION. THERE IS INDEED A HIGH SEAT OF POWER THAT EXISTS FAR BEYOND THE FIELDS YOU KNOW.
MINE OWN JOURNEY SPANS MORE THAN A MILLENNIA, AND NOW IT TAKES ME BACK HOME.

IT WAS NEVER MY INTENTION TO ABANDON ALL THAT WE HAVE CONSTRUCTED.
THE AVENGERS... 'TIS A DREAM I SHARE EQUALLY WITH THEE.
BUT I AM OF TWO WORLDS... AND THE WORLD OF MY BLOOD CALLS TO ME. I MUST HEED THAT CALL.
THIS OCCASION-- 'TIS NOT A HAPPY ONE. SOON I WILL FACE MY HALF-BROTHER UPON THE ROCK OF SKORNHEIM... FOR MINE OWN FATHER HAS DENIED MY WORD AS BOND. HE ALSO REQUIRES PROOF OF MY VIRTUE, AS YOU HAVE...
I...NEVER CONCEIVED THAT SUCH A PLACE COULD EXIST...
IT'S JUST... I'M A MAN OF SCIENCE...
I'M...SORRY I DOUBTED YOU. I PROMISE I'LL NEVER MAKE THAT MISTAKE AGAIN.

MAYBE...I SHOULD JUST TAKE ALL OF THIS AS A *SIGN.*
THE WASP GETTING *SHOT...* CAP OFF ON HIS OWN... NOW *YOU'RE* LEAVING...
NOT TO MENTION... EVERYTHING THAT HAPPENED WITH THE *HULK.* I *STILL* HAVE TROUBLE ACCEPTING THAT I-- THAT *WE*--COULDN'T REIN HIM IN.
I'VE ALWAYS PRIDED MYSELF ON BEING SO *CAPABLE.* SNATCHING VICTORY FROM THE JAWS OF DEFEAT. TURNING A NEGATIVE INTO A POSITIVE. STORY OF MY *LIFE...*
I GUESS I'M JUST NOT USED TO *FAILURE.*
'TIS NO *FAILURE* I SEE BEFORE ME, AVENGER.
ALREADY OUR BAND OF PROTECTORS HAS COME TO *MEAN* SOMETHING TO THE DENIZENS OF MIDGARD. THEY HAVE BEGUN TO *COUNT* ON OUR VIGILANCE...JUST AS WE *HOPED* THEY WOULD.
BUT
URCH--
DO NOT ALLOW THYSELF TO BECOME MIRED IN SUCH *POLITICAL* CONCERNS. OUR ENDEAVORS ARE *BEYOND* THEIR PETTINESS.
THE AVENGERS IS A CONCEPT MUCH LARGER THAN ANY *ONE* MEMBER...YOU OR I INCLUDED. *THAT* IS OUR LEGACY. YOU MUST *NOT* GIVE UP.
I CAN SEE IN THINE *EYES* THAT YOU ARE STILL UNCERTAIN. AND SO I WILL TELL *YOU* WHAT I TOLD OUR FELLOW AVENGER, IN *HIS* TIME OF NEED...
...'TIS ABOUT *FAITH.*
THE STRONGER *YOURS* IS... THE MORE *OTHERS* WILL SHARE IN THY DREAMS.

FARE THEE WELL, MY FRIEND.
DO NOT LET OUR DREAM DIE. FOR THIS *TRUTH* SHALL EVER BE HEARD 'ROUND THE WORLD--
--ONCE AN AVENGER... ALWAYS AN AVENGER!
I GUESS WE'LL *SEE*, THOR...
...IF THERE'S ENOUGH FAITH TO GO AROUND.
OFFICIAL CHARTER
BE IT KNOWN...
That we dedicate ourselves to the establishment, growth and preservation of peace, liberty, equality and justice under
THIS IS OUR SOLEMN OATH.

BOLIVIA
=HMMFGL--!=

RICK!
CAN YOU HEAR ME?!
...HHHNNNN...?
FIRST THINGS FIRST. WE'RE GOING TO GET YOU OUT OF HERE...!
C-CAP...?
THEY... THEY NEVER EVEN...
...ASKED ME ANY QUESTIONS...
...I'M... SORRY, CAP...
SAVE YOUR STRENGTH, RICK. THIS ISN'T ABOUT YOU OR WHAT YOU KNOW--
INDEED.
THE BOY HAS NO CONCEPT OF THE SHEER WEIGHT OF THIS MOMENT...

I'VE WAITED DECADES FOR THIS.
ALL THOSE YEARS...I NEVER ONCE BELIEVED I WOULD BE DENIED MY REVENGE. YOUR RETURN TO THE WORLD WAS DESTINED TO BE...
...ALONG WITH YOUR DEATH AT MY HANDS.
YOU'RE DISEASED, ZEMO.
YOU MURDERED MY PARTNER. IF YOU THINK YOU'RE NOT GOING TO ANSWER FOR THAT--
I AM BEYOND YOUR WORTHLESS JUDGMENTS.
THIS IS YET ANOTHER PRODUCT OF MY SUPERIOR INTELLECT. I SHALL BURN YOU WHERE YOU STAND. BUT NOT BEFORE I SEE YOU BEG FOR YOUR--
I DON'T BEG.
YOUR DEFIANCE ONLY FUELS MY HATRED!
YOURS WILL BE A SLOW DEATH! YOU WILL SUFFER AS I HAVE! YOUR BLOOD SHALL FEED THE SOIL! I SHALL HAVE YOUR HEAD ON A SPIKE!
MY WILL BE DONE!
GO AHEAD, THEN.
TAKE YOUR BEST SHOT.

BREMEN, GERMANY
--THE DETAILS OF REED RICHARDS' NEGOTIATIONS WITH NASA HAVE NOT BEEN MADE PUBLIC.
NONETHELESS, THE FANTASTIC FOUR'S LAUNCH FROM CAPE CANAVERAL PROCEEDED WITHOUT INCIDENT--
--I'VE CHECKEDTHETRAIN SCHEDULESSOIT SHOULDBERELATIVELY EASYTOSNEAK ABOARD--
OH--!
CAREFUL, PIETRO!
MY APOLOGIES, SISTER. IT'S BEEN WEEKS SINCE I'VE HAD PROPER SLEEP. MY JUDGMENT...
I KNOW. THAT'S WHY...WE SIMPLY CAN'T GO ON LIKE THIS...
HIDING IS NO LONGER THE ANSWER. NOT FOR US.
I REFUSE TO LET FEAR DICTATE OUR DESTINY. OUR MUTANT HERITAGE SHOULD BE A SOURCE OF PRIDE--
WANDA!
DO YOU WISH TO GET LYNCHED RIGHT HERE AND NOW?! WE'VE HAD THIS CONVERSATION...
--IN OTHER NEWS ON THE AMERICAN SUPERPOWERED FRONT...
...I SHARE YOUR DESIRE TO STAND PROUD AND SERVE THE GREATER GOOD. TO REDEEM OURSELVES FOR PAST MISTAKES. BUT HOW CAN WE POSSIBLY--
...THE BBC HAS RECEIVED UNCONFIRMED REPORTS THAT ONE OR POSSIBLY SEVERAL MEMBERS OF THE AVENGERS HAVE LEFT THAT ORGANIZATION.
AGAIN, THERE HAS BEEN NO OFFICIAL STATEMENT REGARDING THESE REPORTS...NOR HAS THERE BEEN WORD WHETHER OR NOT REPLACEMENTS WILL BE SOUGHT. PUNDITS ARE SPECULATING THAT THIS MAY INDEED SIGNAL THE END OF THE CONTROVERSIAL TEAM THAT HAS ONLY RECENTLY BEGUN TO GAIN PUBLIC TRUST...
THE END?

OUT OF MY WAY, MAGGOT!
I NEED A CLEAR SHOT--!
JA...
...YOUR END WILL BE MY TRIUMPH...!
CAP!
WATCH IT--!

DRINK DEEP MY FURIOUS RETRIBUTION--!
DAMN YOUR EYES--!
WÜRFEL!
YEEARRGHH--!
LOOKS LIKE YOU MISSED, OLD MAN.
MY VERACHTETER FEIND! YOUR NAME SHALL BE EXPUNGED FROM THE HISTORY BOOKS! YOU AND YOUR WHELP!
EVERY PATHETIC THING YOU REPRESENT WILL BE CRUSHED BENEATH MY BOOT HEEL!
DEATH IS YOUR MISTRESS NOW!

NOT TODAY.
UFFN--!
NEIN--!

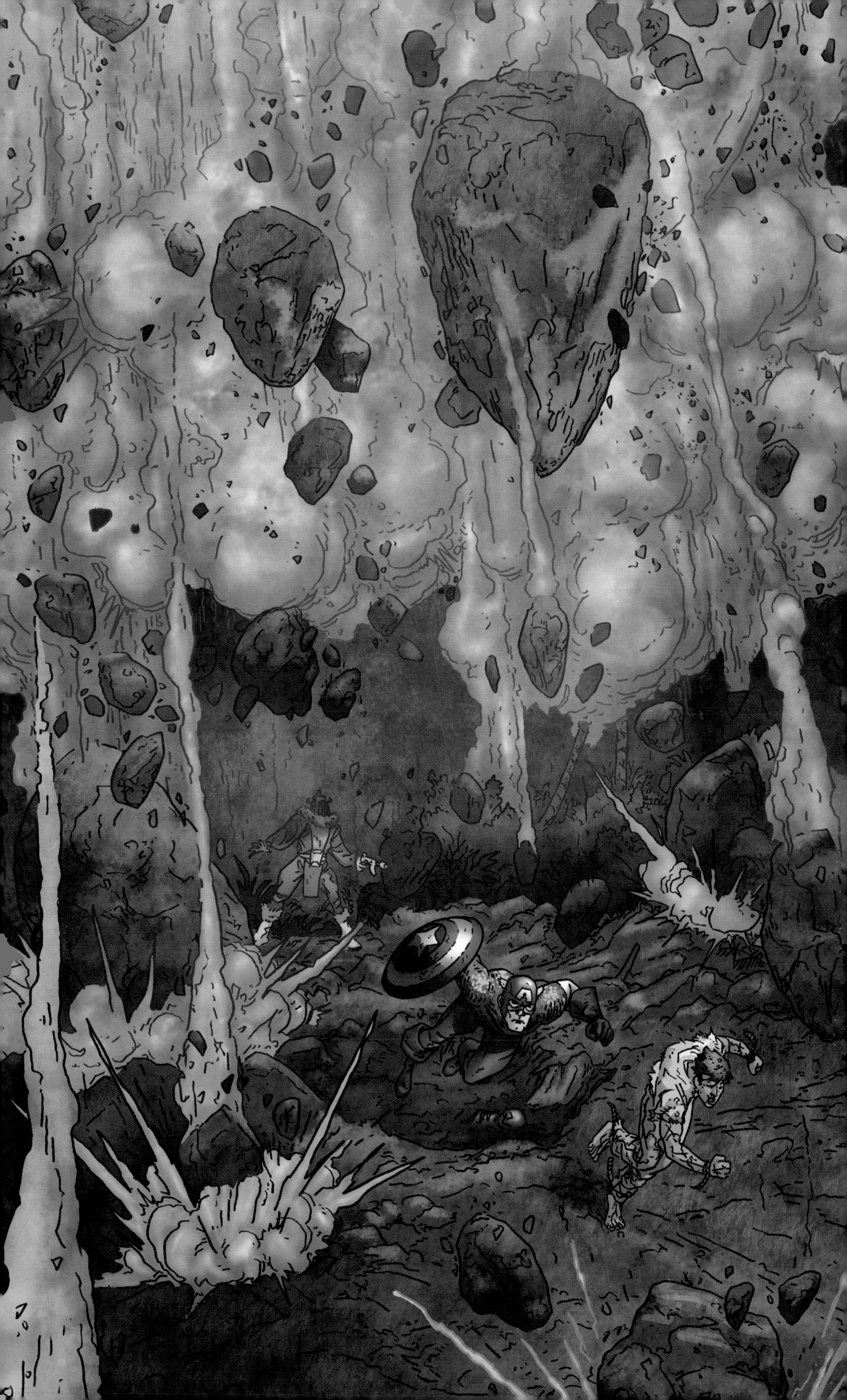

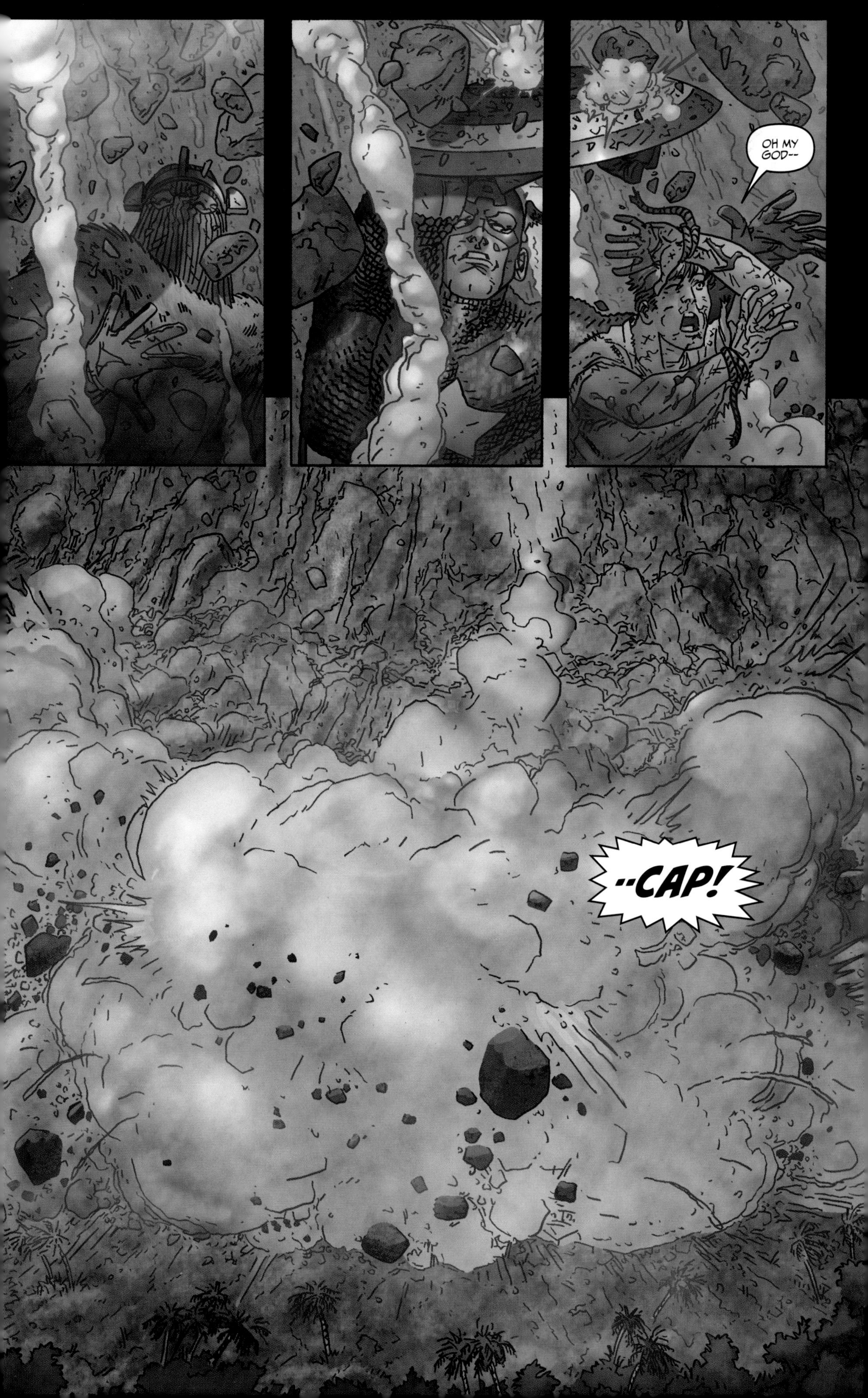
OH MY GOD--
--CAP!

#7
KOLINS 04

AVENGERS MANSION
JARVIS--!
WHAT THE HELL IS GOING ON IN HERE?! ARE YOU--
MMMGGLLFFN--!
≠KAFF--!≠
ALL THIS SMOKE--!
NONE OF OUR PERIMETER ALARMS WERE ACTIVATED. THAT MEANS--
THAT'S RIGHT, PROFESSOR OBVIOUS...
...THAT MEANS YOU'LL NEVER KNOW HOW I GOT IN HERE.
BET THAT DRIVES YOU NUTS.

HAWKEYE.
RIGHT NOW YOU'RE ONLY LOOKING AT A FEDERAL OFFENSE. BUT IF YOU'RE HERE FOR ANOTHER REMATCH, I'LL BE MORE THAN HAPPY TO--
WHOA, WHOA, WHOA...
...I THINK THREE FOR THREE IS ENOUGH FOR ME. I'VE GOT NOTHING TO PROVE IN THAT DEPARTMENT.
FACT IS... I'M NOT WHAT YOU THINK I AM.
AS FAR AS YOUR JANITOR HERE IS CONCERNED...
DON'T DO IT, HAWKEYE--
I'VE GOT HIM, SHELLHEAD. A BOW AND ARROW AGAINST THE THREE OF US...?
DAVID AND GOLIATH, HON. AND THIS DAVID'S GOT MORE THAN A STONE AND A SLING...
...HE'S GOT THREE RAZOR-TIPPED ARROWS AIMED DIRECTLY AT JARVIS! SOMEBODY--
I LIKE THAT ANALOGY.
NOW WATCH AND LEARN, KIDDIES.
STAND DOWN, HAWKEYE. I MEAN IT.
HAWKEYE--

OKAY.
THAT WAS...MILDLY IMPRESSIVE.

LOOK...I TOLD YOU I DIDN'T COME HERE TO FIGHT. I MEANT IT. I WANTED TO TALK...BUT IT'S NOT LIKE I CAN JUST PICK UP THE PHONE AND GIVE YOU GUYS A CALL.
A LITTLE SHOWMANSHIP CAN GO A LONG WAY...
JARVIS! ARE YOU--
I'M...FINE, MA'AM...
YOU AND I HAVE GONE A FEW ROUNDS ALREADY, HAWKEYE. I'VE NEVER DOUBTED YOUR SKILLS. I'VE DOUBTED YOUR CHOICES...
WHAT EXACTLY ARE YOU DOING HERE? AND I'D TALK FAST, IF I WERE YOU...
I'M HERE TO FIND OUT IF THIS LITTLE CLUB IS AS EXCLUSIVE AS YOU MAKE IT OUT TO BE. I'M HERE TO TRY AND DO WHAT I ORIGINALLY PUT THIS MASK ON FOR IN THE FIRST PLACE. YOU GUYS DON'T HAVE THE MARKET CORNERED ON SERVING HUMANITY, Y'KNOW...
HEY, YOU GAVE THE HULK A CHANCE--!
I...UH... WOULDN'T MAKE THAT COMPARISON, IF I WERE YOU...

YOU... WANT TO JOIN THE AVENGERS...
YOU'RE SERIOUS...?
AS A HEART ATTACK. ALL THAT STUFF BEFORE... TO CALL IT A CASE OF "WRONG PLACE, WRONG TIME" REALLY DOESN'T DESCRIBE HOW MESSED UP THINGS GOT. THERE'S A LOT I'D LIKE TO MAKE AMENDS FOR... IF I CAN.
SO, UHHH... WHERE'S CAPTAIN AMERICA...? THOUGHT HE LIVED HERE--
OKAY, LOOK... WE NEED TO TAKE A MOMENT AND PROCESS THIS IN PRIVATE. THIS IS... NEW TERRITORY FOR US.
JARVIS, WOULD YOU MIND...?
N-NOT AT ALL, SIR...
...AS LONG AS HE LEAVES HIS WEAPONS HERE.
NO PROBLEM, JEEVES--
MY NAME... IS JARVIS.
THAT'S WHAT I SAID.
Y'KNOW, I GOTTA ADMIT... I THOUGHT IT'D BE TOUGHER TO GET INTO THIS PLACE. I GUESS IT'S JUST ANOTHER EXAMPLE OF THINGS NOT BEING WHAT THEY SEEM. HOPE YOU FOLKS REMEMBER THAT.
ANYWAY...
...LEAD ON, JEEVES.

WELL, I NEVER WOULD'VE PREDICTED THIS...
...WHO KNEW HAWKEYE HAD A CONSCIENCE...?
OKAY, IRON MAN...WHAT'S THE STORY BEHIND THIS GUY? MORE IMPORTANTLY, IS HE ON THE LEVEL...?
WELL, NOTWITHSTANDING HIS ANTICS HERE TONIGHT, I THINK IT'S STILL SAFE TO SAY THAT HE AND I HAVE HAD A...CHECKERED HISTORY.
WE HAD A FEW RUN-INS AT STARK'S MAIN FACTORY. THE LAST TIME...HE WAS RUNNING WITH A FEMALE SPY. MAYBE HE WAS JUMPING THROUGH HOOPS FOR HER...
I COULDN'T SAY FOR SURE, THOUGH...
CRIMES OF PASSION, EH? I SUPPOSE I CAN RELATE...
SO, HYPOTHETICALLY SPEAKING...COULD HE HANDLE PLAYING WITH THE BIG BOYS...?
I SUPPOSE I SHOULDN'T BE ASHAMED TO ADMIT... HE CERTAINLY HELD HIS OWN AGAINST ME EVERY TIME WE GOT INTO IT.
TRUTH IS... HE'S GOT A FEW SPECIALIZED ARROWS THAT MAKE HIM PRETTY FORMIDABLE.
HMMM...
...WELL, THERE'S A BIGGER ISSUE INVOLVED HERE. I WAS HESITANT TO BRING IT UP, BUT...AS LONG AS WE'RE TALKING OPENLY ABOUT NEW MEMBERS, I THINK WE SHOULD BE HONEST ABOUT WHAT WE'RE REALLY DISCUSSING...
...REPLACEMENT MEMBERS.
MORE SPECIFICALLY... REPLACEMENTS FOR THE WASP AND MYSELF.

I SEE.
I...WAS WONDERING WHEN THIS WOULD HAPPEN. EVER SINCE COUNT NEFARIA--
DON'T DO THAT. DON'T TALK LIKE THIS IS SOME SORT OF INEVITABILITY...
...SINCE DAY ONE, THERE'S NO ONE THAT TAKES THIS MORE SERIOUSLY THAN WE DO. THIS WHOLE THING-- ALL OF IT--THIS IS A DREAM WE SHARE WITH YOU.
BUT AFTER THE WASP... I MEAN...
...SHE ALMOST DIED...!
THIS JOB IS ALL ABOUT RISKING OUR LIVES, GIANT-MAN. YOU KNOW THAT.
THAT'S RIGHT. I DO KNOW THAT. BUT I ALSO HAVE A RESPONSIBILITY FOR THE SAFETY OF MY PARTNER...
THE FACT IS... EVERYONE ELSE HAS BAILED. BUT WE STAYED. NOW WE JUST...NEED TO TAKE A STEP BACK. FROM ALL OF THIS. AT LEAST FOR A LITTLE WHILE...
AND DON'T BLAME HER. THIS WAS MY CALL.
I'M... SORRY, IRON MAN. I WISH THAT--
YOU DON'T HAVE TO EXPLAIN YOURSELF TO ME, WASP. NEITHER ONE OF YOU DO. AND YOU'RE RIGHT. ABOUT THOR... ABOUT CAP...
CAP'S DEFECTION IN PARTICULAR IS GOING TO HAVE THE N.S.C. CRAWLING STRAIGHT UP OUR NOSES. I...START TO WONDER...
...IF THIS IS EVEN WORTH CONTINUING.

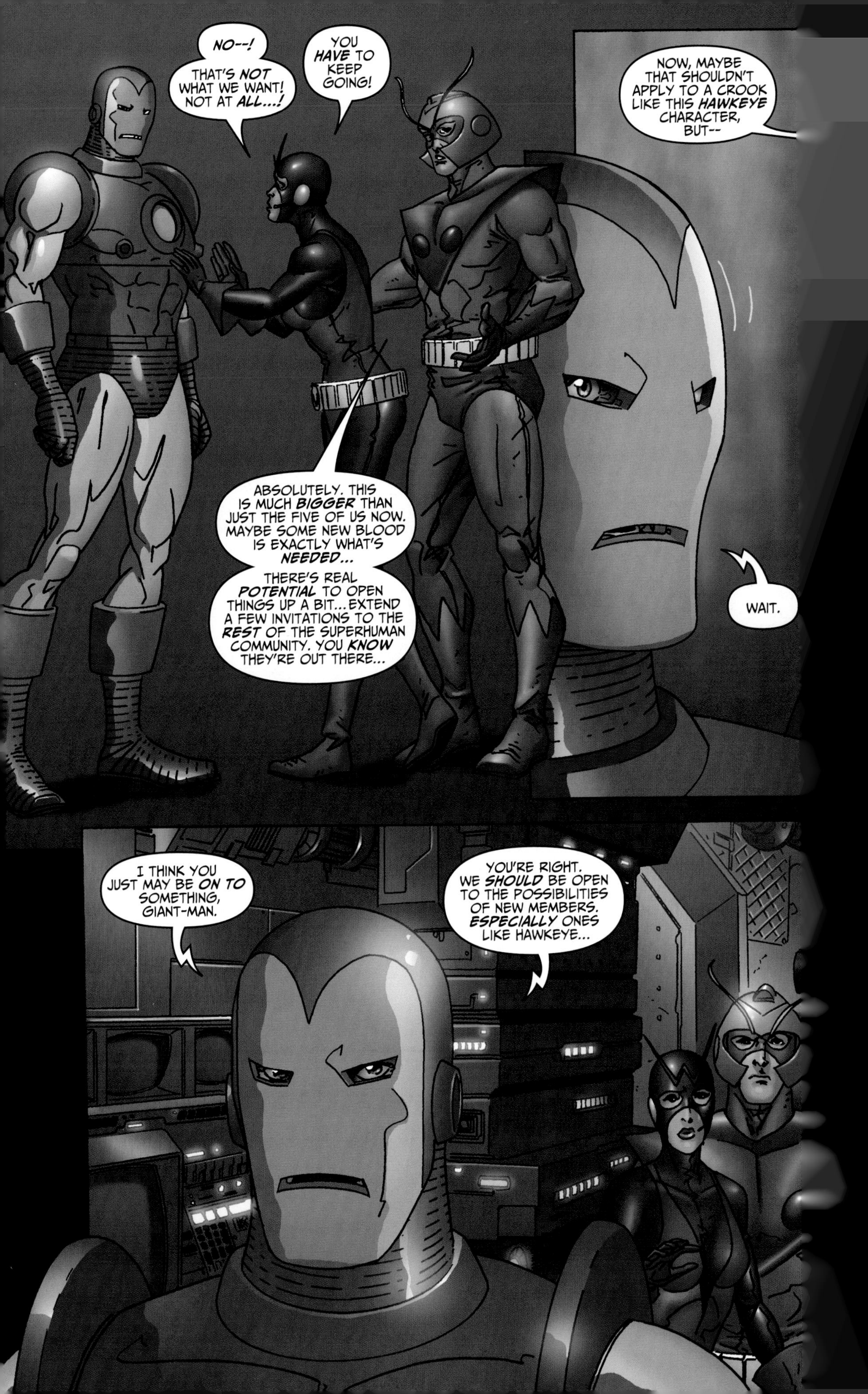
NO--!
THAT'S NOT WHAT WE WANT! NOT AT ALL...!
YOU HAVE TO KEEP GOING!
NOW, MAYBE THAT SHOULDN'T APPLY TO A CROOK LIKE THIS HAWKEYE CHARACTER, BUT--
ABSOLUTELY. THIS IS MUCH BIGGER THAN JUST THE FIVE OF US NOW. MAYBE SOME NEW BLOOD IS EXACTLY WHAT'S NEEDED...
THERE'S REAL POTENTIAL TO OPEN THINGS UP A BIT... EXTEND A FEW INVITATIONS TO THE REST OF THE SUPERHUMAN COMMUNITY. YOU KNOW THEY'RE OUT THERE...
WAIT.
I THINK YOU JUST MAY BE ON TO SOMETHING, GIANT-MAN.
YOU'RE RIGHT. WE SHOULD BE OPEN TO THE POSSIBILITIES OF NEW MEMBERS. ESPECIALLY ONES LIKE HAWKEYE...

WHAT DO YOU MEAN...?
LOOK...ONE THING THAT'S BECOME OBVIOUS TO ME OVER THE LAST FEW MONTHS IS THAT THE AVENGERS AREN'T SIMPLY WATCHDOGS AGAINST THE LARGER THREATS THAT ARISE.
THERE'S MORE TO THIS THAN THE BATTLES WE'VE FOUGHT.
EVERY OTHER HERO--AND WOULD-BE HERO OUT THERE--WE'RE SETTING AN EXAMPLE FOR THE REST OF THEM TO FOLLOW.
WHY ELSE WOULD SOMEONE LIKE HAWKEYE SEEK US OUT...?
YOU'RE NOT SUGGESTING WE TURN THE AVENGERS INTO SOME SORT OF CRIMINAL REHABILITATION PROGRAM, ARE YOU...?
I DOUBT I'D PUT IT LIKE THAT IN THE PRESS RELEASE...BUT WHY NOT?
AFTER ALL, WOULDN'T THAT FALL UNDER THE PURVIEW OF HELPING PEOPLE WHO'RE UNABLE TO HELP THEMSELVES...?
HMMM...
INTERESTING.
THIS IS THE MOST RADICAL IDEA YOU'VE HAD YET, IRON MAN. I THINK THAT'S WHY I LIKE IT...
...BUT WHAT ABOUT THE N.S.C.? NO WAY THEY'LL AGREE TO THIS...
DON'T WORRY ABOUT MURCH.
I'LL HANDLE HIM.

BOLIVIA
CAP...?

WHEN I SAW... THE WHOLE MOUNTAIN COME DOWN...
I MEAN...I THOUGHT YOU'D BEEN--
NO.
JUST ZEMO.
LOOKS LIKE I GOT WHAT I CAME FOR...
EVER SINCE I SAW HIM AGAIN IN MANHATTAN...I'VE BEEN CONSUMED WITH THIS MOMENT. NOT JUSTICE...
...REVENGE.
IT... DOESN'T FEEL LIKE I THOUGHT IT WOULD.

RICK... ARE YOU OKAY...?
OH, SURE... I'M GOOD. N-NO SWEAT.
WHAT ABOUT YOU...? YOU THOUGHT THIS WOULD BE DIFFERENT...?
I SUPPOSE IT'S JUST...
...NOT WHAT I EXPECTED.
'CAUSE YOU'RE BETTER THAN THAT. DON'TCHA GET IT?
LOOK... THIS SCUMBAG KILLED YOUR PARTNER. HE GOT EXACTLY WHAT HE DESERVED... BUT I KNEW YOU'D NEVER ACTUALLY PULL THE TRIGGER...!
I'D BE... MORE CREEPED OUT IF... YOU DIDN'T... THINK THAT...
...NNNN...
...P-PERFECTLY NORMAL...
...H-HUMAN BEHAVIOR...
IT'S ALL RIGHT, SON. I'VE GOT YOU.
YOU FOUGHT HARD. YOU WERE BRAVE. YOU GAVE YOUR LIFE FOR YOUR COUNTRY.
YOU'VE EARNED YOUR PEACE.
GOODBYE, BUCKY.

THANKS, MIA. I'M LIVE IN THE MEDIA ROOM OF AVENGERS MANSION, WHERE A HASTILY ARRANGED PRESS CONFERENCE TOOK PLACE JUST MINUTES AGO.
LIVE - AVENGERS MANSION

THIS IS WHAT IRON MAN HAD TO SAY TO GATHERED REPORTERS...
THANKS FOR COMING ON SUCH SHORT NOTICE. THERE'S A LOT OF RUMORS FLYING AROUND, SO WE THOUGHT WE'D LET YOU AL IN ON THE TRUTH BEHIND RECENT INTERNAL EVENTS.
EARLIER TODAY

PENDING A SERIES OF THOROUGH INDUCTION PROCEDURES AS WELL AS EXECUTIVE CONFIRMATION, WE ARE ANNOUNCING THAT HAWKEYE WILL BE JOINING THE AVENGERS...INITIALLY ON A PROBATIONARY BASIS...

IS IT TRUE THAT HAWKEYE'S GOT A CRIMINAL RECORD--?
ONE AT A TIME, PLEASE...
WHERE ARE THOR AND CAPTAIN AMERICA? ARE THEY--

YOUR PRESS PACKETS WILL DETAIL HAWKEYE'S ST RECORDS, INCLUDING HIS NSC APPLICATION FOR MENCY, ACCORDING TO THE NATIONAL VIGILANTE ACT DEBATED RIGHT NOW IN CONGRESSIONAL HEARINGS.
ALL HE ASKS FROM THE GENERAL PUBLIC...IS A NCE TO PROVE HIMSELF AS THE REST OF US HAVE.

THIS REPORTER HAS LEARNED THAT LAWYERS FRO THE MARIA STARK FOUNDATION ARE ARGUING ANY OUTSTANDING WARRANTS THAT THE BOWMAN MAY HAVE AGAINST HIM, WHILE MATERIALS PROVIDED TO THE PRESS PAINT A VIVID PICTURE OF A POSSIBLY MISUNDERSTOOD HERO...
AND AS THE RANKS OF THE AVENGERS GROW BY ONE, THERE IS SPECULATION THAT MORE CHANGES MAY BE ON THE HORIZON FOR AN ORGANIZATION WITH SUCH A BRIEF-- BUT CONTROVERSIAL-- HISTORY.

ARE YOU INSANE?!

JUST WHO THE HELL DO YOU PEOPLE THINK YOU ARE?!

YOU SCHEDULE A TELEVISED PRESS CONFERENCE TO ANNOUNCE A NEW MEMBER--A KNOWN FELON, NO LESS--WITHOUT CHECKING WITH ME?!
DO YOU HONESTLY THINK YOU'RE OPERATING IN A VACUUM HERE?!
SOMETHING MUST'VE RUSTED IN THAT IRON SKULL OF YOURS! AFTER WHAT HAPPENED WITH THE HULK--!
THE SECOND WE GRANTED YOU A-1 PRIORITY STATUS...YOUR TENDENCIES TOWARD INDEPENDENT THOUGHT CEASED TO EXIST!
YOU CAN'T ALLOW A BLATAN SECURITY RISK ON THIS TEAM!
WAIT... DID I SAY "CAN'T"?! YOU WON'T!
YOU CROSSED THE LINE, MISTER! AND NOW... YOU'RE ALL GOING TO SUFFER THE CONSEQUENCES--! COME TO THINK OF IT...
...MAYBE A SECURITY RISK IS EXACTLY WHAT YOU HAD IN MIND! WHEN THE PRESIDENT GETS THROUGH WITH YOU PEOPLE...!
THAT'S ENOUGH, MURCH.
WHAT DO YOU THINK YOU'RE--?!
YOUR POWER TRIP'S OVER.
IT'S ABOUT TIME YOU UNDERSTOOD WHO'S REALLY CALLING THE SHOTS WHERE THE AVENGERS ARE CONCERNED...

N-NOW WAIT JUST ONE MINUTE--
I'M NOT DONE.
YOU WANT TO TAKE US ON? YOU WANT TO TRY AND PREVENT US FROM DOING OUR JOB? YOU WANT TO INVOLVE THE PRESIDENT IN WHAT I GUARANTEE WILL BE THE MESSIEST PUBLIC RELATIONS NIGHTMARE ANY OF YOU WILL EVER EXPERIENCE?!
BELIEVE ME, THINGS WILL END BADLY...
...BUT NOT FOR US.
IT'S NOT ENOUGH THAT YOU'RE OPENLY DISDAINFUL OF EVERYTHING WE'VE TRIED TO DO HERE... NOW YOU QUESTION OUR MOTIVES?!
AHEM! WELL...
THREATEN ME ALL YOU WANT, IRON MAN. THE FACT IS... THAT PUBLIC TRUST YOU VALUE SO HIGHLY? HOW LONG WILL IT LAST IF YOU'RE ALLOWING CRIMINALS TO SERVE ON YOUR ROSTER?!
YOU SEEM TO FORGET... WE HAD TO EARN THEIR TRUST, JUST LIKE HAWKEYE WILL. I WASN'T LYING DURING THAT PRESS CONFERENCE...!
BY THE WAY... THIS IS JUST THE BEGINNING.
WHAT'RE YOU TALKING ABOUT...?
TWO MORE POTENTIAL RECRUITS HAVE GOTTEN IN TOUCH.
IF YOU THOUGHT HAWKEYE WAS A CURVE-BALL...

LONDON; THREE DAYS LATER
GOOD MORNING. I'M TONY STARK... HERE ON BEHALF OF THE MARIA STARK FOUNDATION, THE ORGANIZATION THAT FUNDS THE AVENGERS.
PIETRO AND WANDA MAXIMOFF... THIS IS SPECIAL AGENT MURCH FROM THE NSC.
I APOLOGIZE FOR THE CLOAK-AND-DAGGER CIRCUMSTANCES. NEEDLESS TO SAY, WE'RE STILL TRYING TO WORK OUT A FEW DETAILS HERE--
SPARE ME YOUR CONDESCENSION, STARK.
I THINK I KNOW EXACTLY WHAT YOU AND THIS GOVERNMENT STOOGE ARE THINKING.
I CAN SEE THE JUDGMENT IN BOTH YOUR EYES--
PIETRO... PLEASE...
STARK... I TOLD YOU...!
ARE YOU REFERRING TO THE MUTANT ISSUE? OR THE FACT THAT YOU'VE BEEN CONSORTING WITH A KNOWN WORLD TERRORIST?
CALM DOWN, PIETRO. I WOULDN'T BE HERE IF THE AVENGERS DIDN'T WANT THIS TO WORK.
WANDA...? ARE YOU--?
I THINK I'M UNDERSTANDABLY NERVOUS, MR. STARK. BUT I--WE--DO APPRECIATE THE STEPS YOU'VE ALREADY TAKEN TO HELP US.

AS FOR WHO WE'VE "CONSORTED" WITH... IT WAS NOT BY CHOICE.
MY SISTER AND I WERE AS TERRORIZED BY HIM AS THE REST OF THE WORLD... IF NOT MORE SO.
FORCED TO COMMIT CRIMINAL ACTS IN THE NAME OF HOMO SUPERIOR... AGGRESSIONS AGAINST HUMANITY THAT WERE NEVER OURS...
WE WERE BORN GYPSIES. WHAT THAT MEANS... IS THAT WE'VE NEVER KNOWN A HOME.
I'M HERE TO FIND OUT IF YOU CAN TRULY PROVIDE ONE. MY SISTER DESERVES THAT.
FOR THAT REASON ALONE, I AM TOLERATING YOU BOTH.
...
RIGHT...
WELL... THAT'S FINE, PIETRO...
OKAY, THEN... WE'VE GOT A BIT OF PAPERWORK TO GO THROUGH HERE...
INSURANCE FORMS... NON-DISCLOSURE AGREEMENTS... PERSONAL INDEMNITIES...
BASICALLY, A LOT OF RED TAPE THAT THE U.S. GOVERNMENT INSISTS ON.

AS PROBATIONARY AVENGERS, YOU'LL BE GRANTED SOME OF THE HIGHEST SECURITY CLEARANCE IN THE U.S., AND THEY DON'T GRANT IT LIGHTLY. SO, WHEN YOU GET A CHANCE... JUST GIVE THOSE DOCUMENTS A--
--READ.
A-HA...
...WELL, YOU MIGHT ALSO BE INTERESTED TO KNOW THAT A GENETICS PROFESSOR OVER AT COLUMBIA VOUCHED FOR YOU BOTH. IS THERE SOME CONNECTION THERE THAT WE SHOULD BE AWARE OF...?
THAT WOULD BE XAVIER. I'M SURE HE WOULD APPRECIATE REMAINING AN ANONYMOUS REFERENCE...
YES, I AGREE.
UHHH... I DON'T THINK IT'S IN YOUR BEST INTERESTS TO BE KEEPING SECRETS AT THIS POINT.
UNLIKE MOST OF THE ROSTER, WE'VE GOT YOUR CIVILIAN IDENTITIES ON RECORD...
...SO IF I WERE YOU--
IF YOU WERE ME, YOU'D ALREADY BE BORED BY HOW AGONIZINGLY SLOW A SPINELESS PENCIL-PUSHER CAN BE WHEN VERBALIZING HIS PARANOIA. YOUR TYPE OBVIOUSLY HAS NO PLACE IN THE COMPANY OF HEROES...
WELL PUT.
OKAY, AGENT MURCH... WOULD YOU MIND EXCUSING US FOR A BIT?
WE REALLY NEED TO GET SOME WORK DONE HERE...
WH-WHAT--?!

SON OF A...
THANK YOU, MR. STARK. THAT MAN WAS...
DON'T MENTION IT. I FEEL THE SAME WAY.
SO, YOU'RE SURE YOU WANT TO KEEP THE SAME COSTUMED IDENTITIES...?
I'M CERTAIN WE COULD THINK OF ALTERNATE CODENAMES--
YOUR CONCERNS ARE VALID, MR. STARK. BUT WE'RE NOT SEEKING PROTECTION...
WE HAVE NO DESIRE TO HIDE WHO OR WHAT WE ARE. NOT FROM HIM...NOT FROM ANYONE.
WHAT WE WANT...IS AN OPPORTUNITY TO SHOW THAT NOT ALL MUTANTS ARE EVIL. THE AVENGERS CAN HELP US DO THAT.
IT'S BEEN A LONG TIME SINCE WE'VE DARED TO TRUST ANYONE. BUT I THINK WE'RE READY TO.
THAT REMAINS TO BE SEEN, SISTER.
OPTIMISM AND SKEPTICISM. YOU TWO ARE QUITE A PAIR.
MAYBE THAT'S WHY I LIKE YOU. AND SO WILL THEY.
"THEY" MEANING THE OTHER AVENGERS, STARK?
LET'S NOT GET AHEAD OF OURSELVES. WE'VE YET TO MEET THEM FACE-TO-FACE...

I'LL BET YOU ENJOYED KICKING ME OUT OF THE ROOM LIKE THAT.
MORE THAN YOU'LL EVER KNOW, AGENT MURCH.
NOT THAT I WOULDN'T PUT IT PAST IRON MAN, BUT ARE YOU TELLING ME THAT THE REST OF THEM ARE FINE WITH HAVING MUTANTS ON BOARD...?!
SO PIETRO WAS RIGHT. YOU ARE PREJUDICED.
I'M SAYING A FRIEND OF MINE HAD A SON THAT WAS KILLED AT CAPE CITADEL!
THOSE TWO WERE RUNNING AROUND WITH THAT LUNATIC MAGNETO FOR MONTHS!
SOUNDS LIKE THEY WEREN'T TOO HAPPY ABOUT IT, EITHER. THEY'RE OBVIOUSLY LOOKING FOR REDEMPTION. SO IS HAWKEYE. WHY SHOULDN'T THE AVENGERS TRY TO HELP...?
MAYBE THEY CAN SUCCEED WITH THESE THREE... WHERE THEY FAILED WITH THE HULK.
PIETRO'S SUPER-SPEED AND WANDA'S HEX POWER... THESE ARE VALUABLE SKILLS IN BATTLE, MURCH. THAT'S THE BOTTOM LINE...
I JUST CAN'T BELIEVE SOMEONE LIKE CAPTAIN AMERICA WOULD AGREE TO ALL THIS...!
PATRIOTISM DOESN'T AUTOMATICALLY EQUAL CONSERVATISM.
CAP'S ALWAYS GONE HIS OWN WAY.
FOLLOWED HIS OWN CONSCIENCE...

TURRIALBA
PETROL
C'MON... C'MON...!
JUST A FRIGGIN' SODA--! IS THAT TOO MUCH TO ASK...?!
APPARENTLY, IT IS.
HOW ABOUT WE JUST DRINK WATER? HEALTHIER FOR YOU.
WATER, SOUTH OF THE BORDER? I'LL PASS.
SO, ANY IDEA WHERE WE ARE...?
ROUGHLY. WE NEED TO FIND A ROAD THAT CUTS THROUGH THIS REGION HERE...
THERE'S AN AIRPORT JUST NORTH OF TORTUGUERO. HOPEFULLY, WE CAN CATCH A FLIGHT STATESIDE...
GOTCHA. THEN WHAT...?
HMMM...?
THEN I TRY TO GET MY LIFE BACK...
...IF THAT'S EVEN POSSIBLE.

LOOK, CAP...
I JUST... WANT YOU TO KNOW...
...WELL, THANKS FOR COMING AFTER ME. I'M...NOT USED TO ANYONE LOOKING OUT FOR ME, SO--
AMERICA... AMERICA...!
USTED ES EL CAPITÁN--! AQUÍ EN EL PERIÓDICO!
OKAY, OKAY...CALM DOWN, MAN...
UHHH...CAP? YOU'D BETTER TAKE A LOOK AT THIS...
AN AMERICAN NEWSPAPER? LOOK AT THE DATE...IT'S ALREADY A WEEK OLD. WHAT COULD POSSIBLY--
USA
NEW AVENGE
Marksman Announc
As Newest Memb
OH.

#8
KOLINS 04

STARK
JFK INTL. AIRPORT
WANDA... PIETRO... WELCOME BACK TO AMERICA.
THE FLIGHT OVER WAS SMOOTH ENOUGH...?
LET ME INTRODUCE YOU TO MY ASSISTANT, PEPPER POTTS. AND THIS IS MY RIGHT-HAND MAN, HAROLD HOGAN. WE CALL HIM HAPPY.
SO, SHALL WE...?
I SHOULD WARN YOU...YOUR ARRIVAL ISN'T EXACTLY A SECRET. WE SIMPLY COULDN'T IGNORE THE P.R. OPPORTUNITY--
I'M NOT SURE WHAT YOU MEAN, STARK. WHO IN THEIR RIGHT MIND WOULD BE INTERESTED IN--
--US...?

THAT
HEM?
--GET A CLEAR SHOT--
WHY AREN'T THEY IN UNIFORM--?!
WATCH OUT, NOW! COMIN' THROUGH...!
QUICKSILVER! SCARLET WITCH! HOW DO YOU RECONCILE YOUR CRIMINAL PASTS--?
MISTER STARK! OVER HERE--!
HOW'S IT FEEL TO BE AVENGERS? WILL YOU BE LIVING IN THE MANSION...?
CAN WE GET A QUICK INTERVIEW--?!
--ARE YOU REALLY MUTANTS--?
MISTER STARK! WHAT DO THE OTHER AVENGERS THINK ABOUT--

CAN WE GRAB A SOUND BYTE FOR THE EVENING NEWS? DO YOU THINK YOU'LL BE ACCEPTED BY THE PUBLIC?
EXCUSE ME...?!
KEEP THAT THING OUT OF MY SISTER'S FACE, OR I'LL BE FORCED TO--

AHHHH...LET'S NOT GET AHEAD OF OURSELVES, FOLKS. THERE'LL BE A FULL PRESS CONFERENCE LATER IN THE WEEK. RIGHT NOW WE'RE JUST TRYING TO GET THEM SETTLED IN.
I WILL SAY THIS, HOWEVER...

...THE AVENGERS ARE MORE THAN PROUD TO OFFER THESE TWO A CHANCE AT A NEW LIFE. A CHANCE TO PROVE THEMSELVES AS HEROES...

...NO DOUBT THEY WILL SERVE AS HONORABLY AS ALL AVENGERS HAVE, PLACING PUBLIC SAFETY ABOVE PERSONAL GAIN.
I, FOR ONE, CAN'T WAIT TO SEE THEM IN ACTION.

THE MAN MAKES QUITE A SPEECH, DOESN'T HE...?
PERHAPS HE SIMPLY DOES WHAT IS NECESSARY TO SURVIVE IN THIS ENVIRONMENT, PIETRO. JUST AS WE DO.

SIX HOURS LATER
SIR? MADAM? IT'S EDWIN JARVIS. I'VE BROUGHT COFFEE.
MAY I ENTER...?
OH...! MY SINCEREST APOLOGIES...!
I HAD NO IDEA YOU WERE STILL... WELL, THAT IS... THAT YOU...
IT'S FINE, MISTER JARVIS...
WE FELT IT APPROPRIATE TO CHANGE INTO OUR UNIFORMS. IF THIS IS TO BE A FORMAL MEETING...
SPEAKING OF WHICH, WHERE ARE THE OTHER AVENGERS? THOR...CAPTAIN AMERICA...
AHHH...BETTER IF THE AVENGERS THEMSELVES ADDRESS YOUR QUESTIONS.
CREAM AND SUGAR, SIR...?
DID THEY SEND YOU IN TO CHECK UP ON US? ARE THEY...UNNERVED BY OUR PRESENCE IN THEIR HOUSE...?
REST ASSURED, YOUNG MAN...THIS IS YOUR HOUSE NOW. AND THE DISTRUST YOU'VE UNDOUBTEDLY EXPERIENCED IN THE OUTSIDE WORLD...
...DOES NOT EXIST WITHIN THESE WALLS.

...DON'T KNOW WHAT THAT GUY WAS TALKING ABOUT. I'VE DRIVEN IN MANHATTAN BEFORE...
SEE? PIECE A' CAKE.
SO THEY GOT THIS NEW GUY ON BOARD. Y'THINK THEY WEREN'T EXPECTING US TO MAKE IT BACK...?
I MEAN, C'MON...! A GUY WITH A BOW AND ARROW--
HOLD ON, RICK...
...LOOK AT THAT.
SOMETHING'S GOING ON UP AT THE MANSION.
WHOA...
CHANNE
7
...WHAT'S WITH ALL THE PRESS COVERAGE?

...REPORTING LIVE RIGHT OUTSIDE OF AVENGERS MANSION AT FIFTH AND SEVENTY-FIRST.
THE PRESS HAS ARRIVED EN MASSE TO FERRET OUT THE TRUTH BEHIND SEVERAL RUMORS CIRCULATING ABOUT THE FUTURE OF THIS SUPER-POWERED ORGANIZATION.
AFTER THE SURPRISE ANNOUNCEMENT OF HAWKEYE'S IMPENDING INDUCTION, MORE NEW RECRUITS ARE RUMORED TO BE RESIDING IN THE MANSION AS WE SPEAK. THIS INCLUDES THE TWO MUTANTS THAT ARRIVED AT JFK EARLIER TODAY.
NO FALSE GODS
THIS RENEWED INTEREST IN THE AVENGERS' ACTIVITIES HASN'T BEEN ALTOGETHER POSITIVE...
...THIS GROUP HAS BEEN CONTROVERSIAL FROM DAY ONE, PARTICULARLY WHEN IT CONCERNS SOME OF THEIR MEMBERSHIP CHOICES.
NORSE MYTH ISN'T CHRISTIA
TAKING INTO ACCOUNT THEIR INCLUSION OF A SELF-PROCLAIMED DEITY AS WELL AS THE HULK'S DISASTROUS INVOLVEMENT...THIS NEW TREND TOWARD ADMITTING REFORMED CRIMINALS HAS A SIGNIFICANT SEGMENT OF THE GENERAL PUBLIC ON EDGE...
MAYBE IT'S JUST A SLOW NEWS DAY...
WISHFUL THINKING, RICK.
WHATEVER'S HAPPENING...WE NEED TO GET IN THERE. AND WE NEED TO DO IT QUIETLY.

LUCKILY, WE'VE GOT A FEW CONTINGENCIES FOR THIS KIND OF CIRCUMSTANCE.
C'MON... YOU FIRST, RICK.
NEVER BEEN DOWN HERE BEFORE...
I JUST DON'T UNDERSTAND WHAT ALL THE FUSS IS ABOUT...
...I HAVEN'T BEEN AWAY THAT LONG...!
HEY, THINGS MOVE FAST THESE DAYS, CAP. YOU'RE STILL ON WORLD WAR II-TIME. THESE DAYS IT'S ALL ABOUT E-MAIL...
I'M SURE IT'S NOTHING. THE PRESS LOVES TO BLOW THINGS UP. GIVES 'EM SOMETHING TO DO. YOU KNOW THAT IT'S PROBABLY BUSINESS AS USUAL UP IN HERE...
CAP...?
WHAT'S...?
I DON'T BELIEVE IT--

--LOOK WHO MADE IT TO THE PARTY!
WELL, CAPTAIN AMERICA...! HOW IS IT THAT YOU ALWAYS SEEM TO SHOW UP AT THE EXACT MOMENT WE NEED YOU THE MOST...?
WHOA...!
I... I DON'T UNDERSTAND. WHO--?

WELCOME BACK, CAP...
...I GUESS WE NEED TO TALK.

OFFICIAL
HARTE
BE IT KNOWN...
at we, the Avengers, ha
nded together to protect a
eguard the Planet Earth,
abitants and resources, fr
y and all threats -- terrestr
otherwise -- which are or mi
ve to be beyond the power
ventional forces to handle.
at we shall brook no interfere
the growth of mankind in
eting its rightful
at we dedicate
ablishment, growth and
servation of peace, liberty,
ality and justice under law.
I OWE YOU ALL AN APOLOGY...
...THE WAY I RAN OFF WITHOUT CONSIDERING THE CONSEQUENCES. I COULDN'T...WELL, THERE'S JUST NO EXCUSE...
I CAN GUARANTEE... IT WON'T HAPPEN AGAIN.
CAP...YOUR HISTORY WITH ZEMO WAS DEEPER THAN ANY OF US WILL EVER KNOW. YOU DID WHAT YOU HAD TO DO.
THE FACT THAT YOU'VE RETURNED SPEAKS VOLUMES.
WELL, I HAVE TO ADMIT, I'M A BIT CONFUSED AS TO WHAT I'VE RETURNED TO...
...I CAN'T BELIEVE THAT THE TWO OF YOU ARE LEAVING...!

I HAVE A FEELING THAT IRONY IS A POST-WAR CONCEPT...
I SUPPOSE...NOT ALL OF US ARE LEGENDARY FOR OUR RESILIENCE. A BRUSH WITH DEATH CAN CHANGE YOUR PERSPECTIVE ON THINGS. BELIEVE ME...IT WASN'T AN EASY DECISION.
I SEE. AND WHAT ABOUT THOR...?
TURNS OUT, HE WASN'T EXAGGERATING ABOUT HIS... THEOLOGICAL HERITAGE.
THERE WERE... OTHER THINGS WHICH EVENTUALLY TOOK PRECEDENCE FOR HIM. I'M ASSUMING HE'S MERELY ON AN EXTENDED LEAVE OF ABSENCE...

I GUESS RICK WAS RIGHT. THINGS CHANGE... SO QUICKLY.
IRON MAN... YOU FEEL CONFIDENT THAT YOU CAN LEAD THIS NEW CONFIGURATION OF AVENGERS...?
NOT EXACTLY, CAP...
THE FACT OF THE MATTER IS... I'M LEAVING, TOO.
YOU'RE... WHAT?!
YOU CAN'T BE SERIOUS! THIS IS YOUR... I MEAN--
IRON MAN...HOW CAN--?
I'M SORRY I DIDN'T TELL YOU TWO EARLIER. I GUESS I JUST...WASN'T ONE HUNDRED PERCENT SURE OF IT UNTIL TONIGHT...
...WHEN CAP SHOWED UP.
I KNOW I STARTED THIS THING. BUT I HOPE I'M NOT SO ARROGANT TO BELIEVE THAT IT CAN'T GO ON WITHOUT ME. IT'S GOTTEN MUCH BIGGER THAN THAT.
IT'S TIME TO PASS THE TORCH...
...TO YOU.

ME...?!
THE AVENGERS NEED YOU, CAP. MORE THAN ANYONE ELSE IN THIS ROOM.
YOU MAY NOT REALIZE IT, BUT SOMETHING SIGNIFICANT HAPPENED WHEN WE DISCOVERED YOU. WE WERE ON THE VERGE OF COLLAPSE. YOUR PRESENCE, YOUR SPIRIT... IT GALVANIZED US.
IT MADE US A TEAM.
UNFORTUNATELY, IT'S MORE THAN THAT... THE GOVERNMENT'S RESTRICTION STILL STANDS. IF YOU LEAVE... THEY'LL STRIP US OF OUR SECURITY CLEARANCE BEFORE WE KNOW WHAT HIT US.
THE AVENGERS' ABILITY TO OPERATE IN THE WAY IT NEEDS TO WILL BE CRITICALLY CRIPPLED.
I...HEAR YOU. I THOUGHT YOU MIGHT BE EXAGGERATING ABOUT THAT BEFORE. I FIGURED, AS LONG AS ANY FOUNDING MEMBER REMAINED, THE N.S.C. COULD BE REASONED WITH. BUT NOW...
...I DON'T KNOW. I MEAN, I NEVER EVEN CONSIDERED THE POSSIBILITY OF LEADING THE TEAM...!
AND THOSE THREE NEW MEMBERS... THEY'RE CRIMINALS...?
I'M AFRAID I NEED TO TAKE SOME RESPONSIBILITY THERE...
I LOOK BACK AT THE SITUATION WITH THE HULK AS MY OWN... PERSONAL FAILURE. I SHOULD'VE MANAGED THAT ONE BETTER. WITH THESE NEW PEOPLE ON BOARD, I... SUPPOSE I SAW ANOTHER CHANCE AT REDEMPTION.
THEIRS AND MINE.

F ANYONE CAN MAKE THOSE THREE INTO AVENGERS, IT'S YOU. F ANYONE CAN CONVINCE THE PUBLIC THAT THEY ARE AVENGERS... IT'S YOU.
THEY TRUST YOU. MUCH MORE SO HAN THEY EVER DID NY OF US. THEY'VE ALWAYS TRUSTED YOU.
FOR THE SAME REASONS THE GOVERNMENT MADE OUR A-1 PRIORITY CONTINGENT UPON YOUR ACTIVE PARTICIPATION.

IDEALISM AND PRAGMATISM. UNDERSTANDING THEIR COEXISTENCE IS THE KEY TO THE AVENGERS' SURVIVAL.
WHAT YOU'RE ASKING... IS DIFFICULT FOR ME TO CONSIDER. FOR OBVIOUS REASONS...
EVER SINCE YOU FOUND ME... I'VE BEEN STRUGGLING TO FIND MY PLACE IN THE WORLD. I'VE MISSED SO MUCH...
...AND I STILL FEEL LIKE A MAN OUT OF TIME.

BUT... YOU ALL GAVE ME A HOME. YOU OFFERED FRIENDSHIP. MOST OF ALL, YOU GAVE ME A PURPOSE. I DON'T KNOW IF I COULD'VE SURVIVED OTHERWISE.

DON'T YOU GET IT, STEVE? YOUR PLACE IN THE WORLD IS HERE.
AS FAR AS I'M CONCERNED, YOU DON'T NEED TO CONFORM TO THE WORLD. WE SHOULD ALL STRIVE TO BE MORE LIKE YOU.

COULDN'T HAVE SAID IT BETTER MYSELF, HON. AND I WOULDN'T BE TOO WORRIED ABOUT ANY OF US LEAVING, CAP...
...AS FAR AS I'M CONCERNED, ONCE AN AVENGER, ALWAYS AN AVENGER.

I APPRECIATE THE SENTIMENTS, MORE THAN I COULD EVER EXPRESS. AND I CAN' IMAGINE THE AVENGERS NOT EXISTING... CERTAINLY NOT BECAUSE OF ANY DECISION I MAKE...
BUT I STILL... I JUST DON'T KNOW...

THOSE ARE THE OTHER NEWBIES...?
SHOULD I KNOW 'EM FROM SOMEWHERE...?
LET'S HOPE NOT...

...I'D HATE TO IMAGINE YOU EVER EXPOSED TO THE HORRORS THEY'VE EXPERIENCED IN THEIR LIFETIMES.

ON THE OTHER HAND, PERHAPS YOU SHOULD SIMPLY TALK TO THEM. YOU MIGHT FIND YOU HAVE A LOT IN COMMON...
...SIR.
RIGHT.

I DIG THOSE THREADS...
...REALLY SHARP. I GUESS SUPER HEROES DON'T USUALLY COMMENT ON EACH OTHER'S FASHION SENSE, HUH...?
EXCUSE ME. IS THIS SMALL TALK OR ARE YOU ACTUALLY TRYING TO OFFER SOME STRANGE COMPLIMENT...?

WOW. I DIG THAT ACCENT, TOO. WHAT IS THAT... LITHUANIAN...?
SO, WHAT... ARE YOU FRESH OFF THE BOAT OR--

WHOA--!
HAVE A CARE, ARCHER. WHEN YOU SPEAK TO MY SISTER, YOU SHOW THE PROPER RESPECT.

OH, I SEE. HER CHAPERONE. UESS THAT'S A FULL-TIME JOB... BEATIN' OFF THE SUITORS WITH A STICK...
ACTUALLY, I'M MENTALLY RUNNING OWN THE LIST OF THINGS ULD BEAT YOU WITH. RIGHT W I'M AT ITEM NUMBER SIX BILLION, TWO HUNDRED-TWENTY MILLION--
FIRST THINGS FIRST, SLICK. YOU NEED TO GET OUTTA MY FACE...
...AND SECOND OF ALL...EXCUSE ME FOR TRYING TO MAKE A LITTLE MAGIC HAPPEN HERE.
GHAD--!
THAT NEVER HAPPENS--!
HOW THE HELL...?!
OH...I GET IT. SCARLET WITCH. HEX POWER. UNPREDICTABILITY.
PERFECT POWER FOR A WOMAN...
LOOK, WE ALL GOTTA WORK TOGETHER, SO I'LL TRY TO KEEP MY HORMONES IN CHECK. FAIR ENOUGH? NO PROMISES, THOUGH...
SO... WHAT'S THE DEAL WITH YOU TWO...?
OUR "DEAL" IS SIMILAR TO YOURS, HAWKEYE...
...MISUNDERSTANDINGS AND RESULTING REGRETS HAVE BROUGHT US HERE. FOR OUR PAST TRANSGRESSIONS, WE HOPE TO SERVE A HIGHER--
NO NEED TO SUGARCOAT THE TRUTH, WANDA. NOT FROM THIS LOUT...
WE'VE BEEN FUGITIVES FOR THE PAST FEW MONTHS. PRIOR TO THAT, WE SERVED IN A TERRORIST ORGANIZATION CALLED THE BROTHERHOOD OF EVIL MUTANTS.
DOES THAT ANSWER YOUR QUESTION...?
BROTHERHOOD OF EVIL MUTANTS.
GOTCHA.
THIS SHOULD BE INTERESTING...

OFFICIAL
HARTER
BE IT KNOWN...
we, the Avengers, have banded togethe
ct and safeguard the Planet Earth,
bitants and resources, from any and all th
errestrial or otherwise -- which are or migh
be beyond the power of conventional f
ndle.
That we shall brook no interference in the g
mankind in meeting its rightful destiny.
That we dedicate ourselves to the establis
growth and preservation of peace, liberty
justice under law.
THIS IS OUR SOLEMN OATH.
FEELS WEIRD OUT THERE...
...EVEN JARVIS SAYS HE'S NEVER HAD SUCH A FULL HOUSE BEFORE.
WHATCHA READING...?
THE AVENGERS CHARTER...
BEEN A WHILE SINCE I'VE LOOKED AT IT...
"...WE DEDICATE OURSELVES TO THE ESTABLISHMENT, GROWTH AND PRESERVATION OF PEACE, LIBERTY, EQUALITY AND JUSTICE UNDER LAW."
THOSE WORDS CARRY A LOT OF WEIGHT...
I KNOW. I'VE READ IT, CAP.
A BUNCHA TIMES...

JARVIS SHOWED THIS TO ME THE FIRST WEEK I WAS HERE.
I'VE BASED MY ENTIRE ADULT LIFE ON THE IDEALS FOUND N THESE KINDS OF IMPORTANT OCUMENTS. THE DECLARATION OF INDEPENDENCE... THE U.S. CONSTITUTION...
...NOW THIS.
YOU MAY BE THE ONLY ONE WHO LIVES BY THOSE IDEALS ANYMORE...
SO I'VE LEARNED. THERE'S NOT MUCH TO DEPEND ON IN THIS WORLD. NOTHING IS SACRED ANYMORE. BUT I SWEAR TO YOU...

...THE AVENGERS WILL BE.

I THOUGHT ZEMO MIGHT'VE BEEN THE END OF MY JOURNEY. TURNS OUT... HE WAS JUST THE BEGINNING.
WISH ME LUCK, RICK. I'VE GOT THREE ROOKIES WAITING WHO NEED A LITTLE GUIDANCE...

YEAH, RIGHT...
...GOOD LUCK.

WELL...
...I GUESS THAT'S IT.
HARD TO BELIEVE WE WON'T BE SHOWING UP HERE FOR THE NEXT WEEKLY MEETING...
I INFORMED MURCH OF THE NEW ARRANGEMENT. HIS RESPONSE WAS MUTED, TO SAY THE LEAST.
ALTHOUGH I COULD HEAR HIM SMILING OVER THE PHONE WHEN I TOLD HIM I WAS LEAVING, TOO...
TO BE PERFECTLY HONEST... I DON'T THINK I'M GOING TO FEEL LIKE SMILING FOR A WHILE...
S-SORRY...
DON'T APOLOGIZE, WASP.
I THINK WE'RE ALL FEELING... A LITTLE AMBIVALENT ABOUT THIS.
...SO I'LL HAVE THE FORMS MESSENGERED OVER. YOU'LL STILL HAVE VOTING PRIVILEGES, BUT I'M ASSUMING THEY'LL WANT TO DOWNGRADE YOUR CLEARANCE LEVEL...
I EXPECTED AS MUCH.
IT'S FINE. WE PLAN ON LIVING LIFE OUT OF UNIFORM FOR A WHILE.
AND IF ALL WE'RE EVER REMEMBERED FOR IS BEING FOUNDING MEMBERS... WELL, THAT'S NOT BAD AT ALL, IS IT?
LOOK, I... WANT TO SAY SOMETHING BEFORE YOU'RE BOTH GONE.
I DON'T BLAME YOU ONE BIT FOR WANTING TO STEP BACK FROM IT. OBVIOUSLY... SINCE I'M RIGHT HERE WITH YOU.

I ALSO KNOW YOU BOTH SACRIFICED A LOT TO HELP MAKE THIS WORK.
THIS IS DEFINITELY A DREAM WE ALL SHARED...
NO DOUBT ABOUT THAT. AND NOW LOOK AT IT... THE DREAM LIVES ON.
PERSONALLY, I REFUSE TO BELIEVE THIS IS THE LAST TIME WE'LL BE SEEING EACH OTHER...
WELL, HERE WE ARE...

I FEEL LIKE A SOLDIER WHO JUST COMPLETED HIS TOUR OF DUTY... BUT WE REALLY DID SOMETHING GOOD HERE. SOMETHING LASTING. HOW MANY PEOPLE CAN CLAIM THAT...?

PLEASURE DOING BUSINESS WITH YOU, GIANT-MAN.
LIKEWISE.

THAT WAS HARDER THAN I THOUGHT IT'D BE.
HANK... DID WE DO THE RIGHT THING...?
PART OF ME FEELS LIKE AN ENORMOUS WEIGHT'S BEEN LIFTED OFF MY SHOULDERS.
ANOTHER PART THINKS... WE MAY BE LEAVING THE BEST PARTS OF OURSELVES BEHIND. YOU'RE ASKING ME IF WE MADE THE RIGHT CHOICE...?

ONLY TIME WILL TELL...

...LET'S JUST HOPE THEY SEND OVER THE PAPERWORK TOMORROW. I WANT THOSE CONTRACTS SIGNED BY THE TIME THE MARKET CLOSES IN TOKYO...
UNDERSTOOD, MISTER STARK.
OKAY, PEPPER. I'LL SEE YOU FIRST THING IN THE MORNING. HAVE A NICE NIGHT.

WELL...?
NOW WHAT...?
OKAY, AVENGERS...
...LET'S GET STARTED.

STARK INDUSTRIES FLUSHING, N.Y.
...INTERESTING TIMES WE LIVE IN, EH, MURCH?
HOW DID YOUR FIRST MEETING WITH CAP GO?
BUSINESS AS USUAL. HE KNOWS PERFECTLY WELL HOW CLOSELY WE'LL BE WATCHING THESE NEW MEMBERS. THIS HAS ALL THE MARKINGS OF A MAJOR CATASTROPHE...
...BUT THE PRESIDENT'S GOT A LOT OF FAITH IN HIM. RIGHT NOW, I'VE BEEN RELEGATED TO CONFERRING WITH THE MARIA STARK LAWYERS ABOUT SUPER HERO STIPENDS AND TAXABLE INCOME.
BUT, AT THE VERY LEAST, YOU'RE MY ADMINISTRATIVE CONTACT...NOT THAT FASCIST BODYGUARD OF YOURS...
RIGHT. I GUESS THAT WOULD BE A COMFORT FOR YOU, WOULDN'T IT...?
HAVE FUN WITH MY TAX ATTORNEYS.
...NEW ERA FOR THIS SUPER HERO ORGANIZATION...
...AS THE PRESS GATHERED TO WITNESS THE OFFICIAL UNVEILING OF THE NEW AVENGERS ROSTER...
...A LINEUP THAT INCLUDES TWO FORMER MUTANT TERRORISTS, ALTHOUGH NEWLY-APPOINTED CHAIRMAN, CAPTAIN AMERICA, WAS QUICK TO ADDRESS THE OBVIOUS CONCERNS...
NEW AVENGERS LINEUP
...THE PUBLIC HAS EVERY RIGHT TO BE WARY OF THIS SITUATION, BUT LET ME ASSURE YOU...
...WE WILL CARRY ON THE PROUD TRADITIONS LAID DOWN BY THE FOUNDERS. WE SHARE THEIR GOALS. WE ONLY ASK FOR THE OPPORTUNITY TO PROVE OURSELVES IN THE SAME MANNER YOU AFFORDED THE ORIGINAL LINEUP.
I PROMISE YOU...

DRAWING DONE FOR ONLINE CONTEST WINNER

COURTESY SCOTT KOLINS

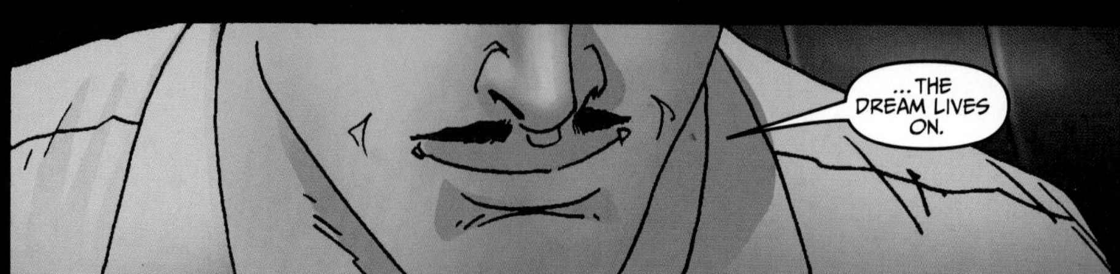

AND THERE CAME A DAY, A DAY UNLIKE ANY OTHER, WHEN EARTH'S MIGHTIEST HEROES AND HEROINES FOUND THEMSELVES UNITED AGAINST A COMMON THREAT. ON THAT DAY, THE AVENGERS WERE BORN -- TO FIGHT THE FOES NO SINGLE SUPER HERO COULD WITHSTAND! THROUGH THE YEARS, THEIR ROSTER HAS PROSPERED, CHANGING MANY TIMES, BUT THEIR GLORY HAS NEVER BEEN DENIED! HEED THE CALL, THEN -- FOR NOW, THE AVENGERS ASSEMBLE!

THE BEGINNING